do i look

look

fat

in this?

Life Doesn't Begin Five Pounds from Now

by JESSICA WEINER

POCKET
BOOKS

LONDON • SYDNEY • NEW YORK • TORONTO

First published in Great Britain
by Simon & Schuster UK Ltd, 2007
A CBS COMPANY

Originally published in 2006 by
SIMON SPOTLIGHT ENTERTAINMENT,
A Division of Simon & Schuster, Inc.
1230 Avenue of the Americas
New York, NY 10020

1 3 5 7 9 10 8 6 4 2

Simon & Schuster UK Ltd
Africa House
64–78 Kingsway
London WC2B 6AH

www.simonsays.co.uk

Simon & Schuster Australia
Sydney

A CIP catalogue record for this book is
available from the British Library

ISBN-13: 978-1-4165-2592-9
ISBN-10: 1-4165-2592-0

Printed and Bound in Great Britain by
Cox & Wyman Ltd, Reading, Berks

CONTENTS

Conversion chart of women's dress sizes

US	UK	AUS/NZ	CONTINENTAL
4	6	6	34
6	8	8	36
8	10	10	38
10	12	12	40
12	14	14	42
14	16	16	44
16	18	18	46
18	20	20	48
20	22	22	50

INTRODUCTION

"Do . . . I . . . Look . . . Fat . . . in . . . This?"

I had to spell it out for him. He—my new, supercute, and very loving boyfriend—had no idea about the tornado that had just blown through my self-esteem. I was getting ready to attend his cousin's wedding, and as I was zipping up my dress, the zipper broke, leaving me to come to the only rational conclusion possible: I was *too fat* to go to a wedding, enjoy myself, have a good time, or be remotely worthy of love. Ever. The end. I am so gross.

Those thoughts floated through my head on a regular basis, just looking for a reason to spill out of my mouth. And spill out they did, as my boyfriend sat there—fully dressed and content—flipping through the channels on the hotel TV. We were in rural Pennsylvania, so there wasn't much of a choice, but I guarantee that whatever he was watching (skeet shooting, I believe) was way more interesting than watching me do my body-loathing dance.

The busted zipper was just adding insecurity to my day. I was meeting most of his extended family for the first time that evening. And now I had nothing to wear and no time to fix the zipper. He suggested that I just put on something else I had packed. Hmmm . . . like what? The cloud-and-lamb-covered flannel pajamas I had packed in case his mother walked into our hotel room? I had no other clothing appropriate to wear to a wedding/meet-the-family event, and I was a wreck.

I kept asking him the same question—"Do I look fat in this?"—while modeling the completely broken dress. I don't know what I was waiting for. For him to say, "Yes, honey, you look like a huge fat cow and I can't believe I am introducing you to my family"? Or, "Yes, babe, truth be told, your flabby ass busted right through that zipper. Next time try putting on a girdle before zipping up"? I mean, really, what did I expect? And besides, no matter what he might say to me, it would never rival the disgusting, self-mutilating thoughts I had going on in my head. If there were such a thing as a "terror alert" for poor body image, mine would have been elevated to emergency status: red for "stop her before she ruins this relationship with her insecurity!"

I watched his face turn and twist and contort itself into all sorts of expressions as he tried to compute an answer. See, my sweetie was a scientist, and I'm sure he was completely baffled by the fact that there was no straightforward, calculated, easy, breezy way to answer me. So instead, he just stared at me and smiled. Lovingly. Of course, this only made it worse. Way worse. Because in my sick, twisted mind I thought he was laughing at me and at my broken-zipper fatness.

And then he scooped up my crushed ego from the floor—where I had slithered down to form a total body mush pile—and suggested we go to the nearest department store to try to find a substitute outfit. Exhale. Yeah, I guess that could work.

So we went, and I found a very suitable dress. In fact, I loved it way more than the original choice, and my spirits were lifted, with at least some semblance of sanity sneaking back in. And my boyfriend felt like a hero. He had thwarted an epic disaster and still had time to get back to the hotel to finish watching the skeet-shooting competition. I put the finishing touches on my hair, fixed up the mascara that had been washed away by my tears, and went to meet the family.

• • •

"Do I look fat in this?" It is perhaps the most dreaded question in modern relationships. At some point our partners, boyfriends, and husbands learn to expect this question, as if we have some sort of horrible body-image Tourette's syndrome. We are most likely unaware of how many times during the day we assault our loved ones with this insane and unanswerable question.

The episode in the hotel room wasn't the first or last time I uttered those six words to someone who loved me. And I would continue to use them against myself and toward others until I realized that those six little words mean so much more than we initially understand. They are part of a secret language: the Language of Fat. It's a language most women speak. We whisper it to our girlfriends, shriek it to our boyfriends, and say it to just about anyone who will listen.

In our desperation to engage in the Language of Fat, we use the phrase "Do I look fat in this?" as a greeting, a question, a salutation, and a general tribal warrior cry to other women when we are looking for bonding and support.

If I knew then what I know now, I would have spared my boyfriend the agony of having to entertain such a ridiculous question that day back in that hotel room. I would have understood that my freak-out was not about the zipper breaking (which happens, by the way, when you buy a vintage dress from a used-clothing store). It was really about my fear that his family wouldn't approve of me. It was my old belief system kicking into gear, the voices that told me that in order for me to be appreciated, I should look like I just popped off of a magazine cover . . . perfect! Not an imperfect, flawed, nervous, crazy-in-love woman who wants to do the right thing and have people love her. Nope. Just being myself wasn't good enough.

Today, if I listen closely, I can identify you by the language you speak. In one sentence I can know that you are one of us, part of the tribe of body haters, speaking the Language of Fat to anyone who will listen. And maybe you don't even realize you're doing it. Perhaps this bonding ritual is so ingrained in your daily life that you walk around completely dissatisfied and you don't know why.

Those of us who speak the Language of Fat are everywhere. We are:

- The twelve-year-old girl who pulls at her low-rise jeans as her belly hangs over the waistline, wondering if she will ever be thin like the popular girls.
- Your beloved boyfriend, who spends an extra hour each night doing sit-ups because he can't control the belligerent boss he does battle with every day at work.
- The high-powered executive who, after catching sight of her reflection in the mirrored glass buildings on the way to the office, pledges to begin yet another diet on Monday morning.

- A mother yelling at her daughter because she broke the "rules" by eating a piece of bread while the whole family is on a no-carb diet.

- Your best friend, who always lends you a shoulder to cry on but inside feels that *her* shoulders, arms, and the rest of her body are just too fat to deserve love in return.

- The pretty, skinny girl asking everyone around her if she is fat, because she doesn't know how else to communicate her need for comfort and connection.

- The elementary school teacher who doesn't bring a lunch to school and goes hungry during recess.

- The Hollywood actress high on a pedestal, admired for what she looks like, who is really starving, literally, for permission to just be herself.

- The panicked grocery store shopper who loads up her cart with trendy diet foods, none of them anything she really wants to eat.

- A new mother who spirals into anorexia and bulimia while trying to lose her baby weight—fast.

- A group of girlfriends who, when they greet one another, always say, "You look great, have you lost weight?"

- Yet another fabulous woman full of guilt, eating ice cream and contemplating plastic surgery while watching the latest makeover/dating reality show.

- Me, wasting precious years of my youth despising my form and forsaking my curves, in favor of and in search of a body that just looked like someone else's.

- You, who hoped that by picking up this book you would, just for one second, better understand why you dislike your body so much.

Out of my own recovery a career was born. For the past fourteen years I have had the chance to speak and hold workshops across the United States, visiting with thousands of people in their dorm rooms, boardrooms, and living rooms, discussing this pervasive and distracting language. Many of the people I work with e-mail their stories and ask for help and guidance in translating the Language of Fat in their lives. As someone who has lived through the destructive and damaging impact of this language, I am well aware of how easy it is to believe that your worth is tied up in your weight or body size. The Language of Fat is a language most women are taught to speak in this country. It is its own separate communication that women first learn as children and then cultivate as they mature in life. We sprinkle this language into our everyday dialogue like it is a zero-calorie condiment.

"Do I look fat in this?" doesn't mean what you think it means. It is actually code for *Help!* "Please help me, something is terribly wrong in my life. I feel like shit. Worthless. Hopeless. Scared. Overwhelmed. Confused."

Or it can be code for *Pay attention to me!* "I am desperate to be loved, need your approval, or want your affection."

Or it can be code for *I am trying to fit in.* "I want to be your friend, I am just like you, trust me and confide in me!"

It can mean a hundred things, and all of them are more than what it sounds like. This language leaves in its wake millions of women who feel unfulfilled in all areas of their lives, and it impacts millions of men and best friends, who are forced to find an answer to an unanswerable question.

What we haven't realized yet is that this body insanity doesn't end with the rage you feel toward your stomach, the disapproval of your upper arms, the disgust you find in your thighs and calves. *The way you feel about your body affects your entire life*. It impacts your health, wealth, family, relationships, and career. It doesn't stop with the embarrassment you feel for your breasts, or the hatred you have for your nose, chin, or thighs. Those are just the obvious ways we communicate something much deeper: a lack of passion, a longing for love, and a severe absence of self-esteem.

Bathroom Babe

Throughout my career I have experienced some intimate and powerful exchanges with women. Anyone who knows me knows of my karmic relationships with bathrooms. For some reason these are the places where I meet the most interesting people and experience the most life-changing events. Even the impetus to write this book came from a bathroom bonding session I had in a Manhattan bookstore a few years ago.

I was applying the finishing touches to my lip gloss in the tiny bookstore bathroom, which boasted only one stall and a larger than life fluorescent light that kept blinking and threatening to turn off at any minute. I was gearing up for an afternoon discussion and book signing for my first book, *A Very Hungry Girl*. In a few days I would be embarking on a four-month book tour that would take me across the country and connect me with thousands of amazing people and their stories. I was experiencing a roller coaster of emotions—equal parts trepidation, pride, elation, and terror. "Will people get it?" "Will people like it?" "Will people buy it?"

After two more coats of lip gloss were added to my already shiny lips, a woman entered the bathroom to wash her hands. We squeezed side by side to share the mirror, and I noticed that she was staring at me. I met her stare with one of my own. "I'm sorry, you look familiar to me. Oh, wait," she said. "You're the author speaking today. That's where I know your face—I just saw the sign with your picture on it!"

"Yes, that's me," I responded, surprised.

"Is this your first book?" she asked.

"Yes, it is!"

"Wow, how exciting. Are you going to write any more? Do you know what your second book will be about?" She went on, asking me more questions, but my mind was frozen in time with this one.

What? What *are you asking me?* I thought. *I'm about to deliver the first of many first book signings relating to my first book ever, and you're asking me about my second? Are you crazy? Oh my gosh, the pressure . . .* And then, interrupting my drama queen moment, came a sweet dose of reality.

She had moved on from inquiring about my dreams and intentions for a second book, and instead had focused on her thighs. "Well, maybe I'll write a book someday, once I lose this weight. I tell you, I keep carrying around this extra ten pounds right here on my thighs." And with that she reached down to grab a piece of her thigh and show me the culprit that she per- ceived was covering up her aspirations and ambitions.

You'd think that this kind of random intimacy between women in a bathroom would scare me off or make me think twice. But nope, not me. Women, whether they are a size two or twenty-two, feel this kind of body-loathing and obsession. I have seen it manifested everywhere, from bathrooms to boardrooms. Women of all sizes always have something to say about their bodies. And I always find myself on the receiving end of these kinds of admissions.

In a superhero world my title would be "Bathroom Babe," able to leap bathroom stalls in a single bound and rescue the tormented body haters who inhabit the ladies' rooms across the world, pinching, pulling, twisting, and mutilating their bodies into submission.

I can meet a woman in the bathroom and we can talk about the size and shape of our thighs before we even know each other's names.

We can become momentary best friends bonding over who has more cellulite, who feels uglier, who's having a more terrible hair day. We can get into gory detail over how these jeans make our butts look big or our hips look huge, before we have even finished drying our hands. And we don't dare put on the last dab of lip gloss before we grumble under our breath, the first and last words in our deadly dance of body-loathing, "Do I look fat in this?"

Think about it. Isn't it odd that before I could know anything else about you, like your name, what you do for a living, what kind of dreams you have, or what your favorite color is, I'm privy to the relationship you have with your body? Why is it that you and I speak this crazy language? How can it change or destroy our lives if we let it? And what can we do about it?

I am going to share with you stories, advice, and ways to begin to build a better way of communicating. We are going to decide once and for all to discard the legacy of loathing passed down to us by parents, friends, advertisers, and the media.

I will show you how the language we speak in everyday life, even the seemingly simple question "Do I look fat in this?" is sabotaging your happiness and your well-being in your health, wealth, family, relationships, and career.

The following chapters will begin with a commonly used phrase found in the Language of Fat and will break down its meaning, usage, and translation. Then I will share with you my insights and personal stories about using the very language we will soon banish from our lips. I will include some questions that have been sent to me over the years, as well as some illustrative stories, and I will wrap up the chapters with advice, tools for change, and action steps. Please note that although I have changed names and identifying details of those portrayed—and in some cases created composite stories—the questions and stories presented here are all based in truth, and are emblematic of the sentiments shared with me time and again.

Over the past few years I have coined the term "Actionist" to describe what I do and the kind of life I lead. An Actionist is someone who is willing to take action in his or her everyday life. It doesn't mean you have to burn your bras or protest in Washington. It doesn't mean you have to have all the answers or a fancy education. It just means that you are someone who inspires others by walking your talk. Someone who is brave when scared, bold even when it isn't fashionable, and always has an eye toward self-responsibility.

By the end of this book you will realize that your life is created by the thoughts you think, the language you speak, and the actions you take.

Your life begins now, not five pounds from now!

Chapter One

Decoding the Language of Fat

F-A-T

Who would have ever thought that three little letters could cause such fear, anxiety, and pain in someone's life?

I don't know one person who is not affected by those three letters. I don't know one woman who has *never* had a thought about how much she weighs or whether she is, or is getting, fat. Unless you're from a faraway planet called Self-Love, you grew up in a world where women are still valued, honored, rewarded, validated, and appreciated based on the size and shape of their bodies.

You can have the best parents, the most prestigious education, the most loving partners, the greatest friends, and you, my love, will still be susceptible to equating your worth as a woman to your dress size. And this isn't a new realization. We have always loved and hated women based on their beauty and their physical stature, and we have always loved and hated ourselves based on how easily (or not) we have lived up to these standards of womanhood.

Waiting to Be Skinny

I recently met a brilliant young woman at an Ivy League conference on women's issues. She had just graduated magna cum laude from her school, but she confided that she couldn't remember a damn day of her college experience. "Why?" I asked, utterly shocked at this statement. "Because," she said, "I have been waiting till I was skinny to enjoy my life. And it hasn't happened yet, so while I just finished my education at one of the country's most prestigious schools, I can't remember anything about it because I was too busy dieting, hating my body, and waiting to be skinny."

Are you waiting to be skinnier, thinner, more toned, more tanned, better dressed, more lovable, sexier, nicer, smarter, funnier, or wealthier before you really begin your life? Millions of us are. And it's a complete waste of time. Body obsession and the quest for perfection are destroying our lives, and we are willing partners in this destruction.

F-A-T = Feelings. Action. Thoughts.

That is how I've translated the word "fat." Feelings, action, thoughts. It reminds me that we are just speaking two different languages. The Language of Fat is the overall title for a general sense of uneasiness and dissatisfaction in our lives. We are not fulfilled in our jobs, relationships, friendships, or self-esteem, so we focus on the external—because that seems more within our realm of control and influence. We have to think about what's going on inside, too.

?? **Take This Quiz** ??????????????????????

- How many times today have you thought about what you ate or want to eat?
- How many times have you used the word "fat" in a sentence?
- How many times have you thought about the word "fat," whether about yourself or someone else?
- How many times today have you dreamed of a life that would happen five pounds from now? (When you finally get thin. Or when you get a new husband or boyfriend. Or when you have the perfect job. Perfect friends. Perfect family.)
- How many times today did you let the Language of Fat seep into your experience?

Odds are that if you were able to answer any of the questions above, you are speaking the Language of Fat and may not even know it.

The Language of Fat

Your health, wealth, family, relationships, and career are all affected by the Language of Fat and how you speak about your body. It seeps into other areas of your life because body image is about your self-image and about how you imagine your life should be.

The Language of Fat is about more than the word "fat." It is about more than just the fear of becoming fat. It is the nagging, brutal voice in your head that says your life isn't worth living until you look a certain way.

Remember, your life is worth more than the number of calories you eat during the day. Or the number of times you run around the track. You should design the life you desire. And before you can do that, you have to look at what's been holding you back, informing your decisions and opinions.

No one is immune to the power of this language. And it will take a collective effort from people willing to take action in their everyday lives to shift this language, to decode it, deconstruct it, and put a new language in its place. That's what we'll try to do together in this book.

What Happened to Penny

The word "fat" became a weapon to me when I was in grade school. It was the word girls used to wound one another. And it was the worst reason for rejection from a guy. It was the ultimate and most decimating cut-down. Nobody wanted to be called fat. Not the kids who really were or the girls who never would be. "Fat" could mean a lot of things. Undesirable, messy, ugly, out of control, stupid, lazy, unpopular. Once you were called fat, it stuck with you like gum on your shoe; you might be able to get the majority of it off, but there would always be a trace of the sticky stuff there.

For girls it meant complete girl failure. I remember seeing a gaggle of prepubescent girls circle a new student named Penny, who had just blown us all out of the water with her perfect score on a spelling test. She was smart and she knew it—a deadly combination for those of us already hating ourselves at an early age. Girls with poor self-esteem can smell confidence like dogs smell fear, and then the mission is clear: Do your best to destroy the girl in the group who actually likes herself.

And so they formed a circle around Penny one day after gym class and unleashed upon her the most devastating of offenses: "Penny is so . . . fat." It was simple, and it did the trick. Penny became pegged as the girl with a weight problem. The girl who was smart but fat.

The only time Penny had the chance to reverse her girl curse of being fat came when she had stayed home from school for a week because she had flu. When she returned, she had lost a lot of weight. There was no way anyone could call Penny fat without looking really lame. Penny relished her new post-sickness body for a few days, but soon she began to return to her normal self. And then the teasing resumed. Because, in the hierarchy of the preteen world, once a group finds its "fat victim," it sticks with him or her until all torment and torture are complete.

The crazy thing about this story is that I can't even tell you if Penny actually had a weight problem. Not that it really matters, anyway. But I don't remember what Penny looked like; she was just the smart new girl in class who got a perfect score on her spelling test. However, as soon as the fat blanket was thrown on her, all I remember is her embarrassment at becoming a social pariah.

Forty percent of elementary school girls are on a diet.

Thou Shalt Not Be a Fat Woman . . . Ever!

How old were you when you first heard the word "fat"? When did it become the very thing you designed your life around *not* becoming?

We are socialized early on to understand that girls should want to be slim and pretty, not fat and ugly. Seems logical, right? Who in her right mind wants to be fat and ugly? But what is missing in these descriptions are the millions of other things we can be in our lives.

Let's get smart about this. The Language of Fat is not really just about the word "fat." It starts with this word, the most emotionally recognizable word for women in this country, and it spreads into other words, into a deeper and sometimes more subtle language that can keep us from ever knowing we are speaking it.

The girls who torment other girls probably don't even realize they've been fed a steady diet of body-loathing terms in their young years on this earth. Before we understand the meaning of a word, the energy associated with the response it brings has an impact on us. The girls know that the word "fat" is just something no girl wants to be. They've probably heard their mothers say it, perhaps when getting dressed or preparing dinner. Maybe they've heard their mothers ask their fathers or stepfathers, "Honey, do I look fat in this?"

No matter how, they learned it. They mimicked it. Now they use it and they watch it get them results. They may continue to speak the Language of Fat every day and may spend their lives poking, prodding, and praying never ever to become fat themselves.

Remember, the fear of being fat isn't only relegated to women with preexisting weight problems. The notion of not becoming fat occupies a lot of time and space for women of all shapes and sizes.

Becoming fat is a realistic fear for women, one that controls entire lives and millions of daily activities. This is not uncommon; all women have some sort of fear about this issue. It's almost like it's one of the Ten Commandments, or a federal law.

It's a Bonding Thing

Most likely, no one's ever told you that you don't have to speak the Language of Fat. Women bond with this language, and through the bonding we send the message that this kind of thought process and obsession is normal. We are normalizing body hatred in this country by continuing to speak the Language of Fat.

The fear of becoming fat may be irrational, but it causes you much stress in your life—and the lives of those around you—because you continue to speak the Language of Fat.

What does being "fat" mean to you? What does it mean in your relationships? In your career? In your family? What would happen to you if people perceived you as fat?

Decoding the Language of Fat is not rocket science. It is about listening—to yourself and to others—and asking deeper questions. The notion of "fat" means different things to different people. "Fat" can be a catchall phrase for many other emotions. It's much easier going through the world as a woman saying, "Ooh, I don't want to be fat," rather than, "I am frightened of being unloved or abandoned." Hearing the first of those statements, we all nod our heads in knowing approval, but at the second statement we run in the other direction—because the poignant fear feels all too real.

Step One: **Cutting the Fat**

The good news is, we have power over the Language of Fat. We can dissect it, understand it, and then choose to change it so it no longer takes over our lives. The first step, though, is to recognize that you speak it. The next step is to be willing to do something about it.

• You can challenge the language by looking beyond the words and actions and into the intentions. Sometimes it is so easy to stick with the status quo and not rock the boat by asking, "Is this language really the best use of our time?" The feeling of being left out of the group is overwhelming. But we don't have to speak in surface dialogue about food, fat, or weight. There is so much more to talk about and to bond over.

• You don't have to speak the Language of Fat just because it is the predominant language.

• Keep listening.

• Language habits won't change overnight, but you can begin to change yours immediately just by being aware.

Young Girls Are More Afraid of Becoming Fat Than They Are of Nuclear War, Cancer, or Losing Their Parents

Dear Jess,

My daughter is ten and overweight. She gets teased a lot at school for being "fat" so I try not to use the word "fat" around her at home.

Instead, when we talk about her weight, we talk about her not wanting to be "pudgy" or "chubby." Are those better words to use?

—Rita

While I applaud Rita's effort to try to choose nondamaging words to share with her daughter, the new words she's chosen mean essentially the same thing. Just because you aren't saying the word "fat" doesn't mean you aren't passing on the fear of becoming fat. Even though Rita uses other words, they still carry the notion that there is something wrong with her daughter. Rita wants to make sure her child is not teased by others and is the healthiest little girl she can be. So she must be extra diligent in the language she uses, especially with her daughter.

We have to talk to kids in terms of inner value and not outer appearance. The most important approval for any child is from his or her parents. Fill children up with other descriptive terms: loving, witty, smart, kind, sincere, sensitive, bubbly, funny, strong, and heroic. We can never hear enough of those words.

You Are Your Toughest Critic

Worrying about any aspect of your appearance to the point where it is alienating friendships and relationships is problematic. Some of us haven't yet learned another way to communicate our needs. Incessant worrying about how you look and what other people think of you isn't vanity as much as it is a way for you to keep yourself powerless and playing the victim. When you evaluate your self-esteem and self-worth based on what others think of you or on group approval, you essentially give up anything unique and individual about yourself. You are, in fact, wasting a lot of time by focusing on approval from the outside world.

This sort of constant worrying and insecurity takes a toll on friendships. We like to have friends who can also give us something in return. Are you able to be there for your friends, or are you too busy hijacking the conversation, asking them if they think you're pretty? If I were your friend, I would want you to enjoy being the person I became friends with in the first place. And I would need you, as my friend, to be present and alert in our relationship. Consider the following:

- How much time is wasted in your life feeling insecure, needy, and focused on appearances?

- How much time is spent on enjoying your life, being with friends, and discovering more parts of you?

- How much of your time with friends is spent on asking them to reinforce your self-esteem, or on them asking you to reinforce theirs?

Perfect Doesn't Exist

People can tell you that you're the prettiest girl in the world, but that won't make you any more secure.

Who sent the memo to girls that it would be our responsibility to grow up hating how we look or worrying so much about what other people think? It shouldn't be this way, and it doesn't have to be! You can choose to no longer be tied to dieting and self-loathing. It will take courage to create another way of looking at yourself and the world, but it's worth it. No one really has a perfect life. Everyone is struggling with something in his or her own way. The answers don't lie in what you are eating or not eating or how much you are working out. The answers are not found in celeb magazines or the greener grass of Hollywood. If you don't feel like you are living the life you want, you have to be willing to do something to change that. The change won't come from an external validation or a magic diet. The world is wide open to what you have to offer. (If your sense of being unfulfilled has led to feelings of depression or hopelessness, I suggest seeking some professional help as well.)

You have to play an active part in this world by putting your time and energy into being the best version of you.

Obsession with diets and exercise programs is common among women. We feel in control when we diet, but that feeling is false and fleeting. Dieting is the biggest culprit in the Language of Fat. It starts us on a journey of shame, blame, guilt, and restriction. I do believe in finding a balance for yourself in life, where you are moving and feeding your body so that you feel strong, vital, and clear. But the ultimate goal should be clarity and peace—not a certain size or number on the scale.

Can We Change the Subject, Please?

Dear Jess,

Sometimes I want to scream!! If I hear one more beautiful woman say she is ugly or fat again, I might just hurt someone!! All of my hot, attractive girlfriends think they are ugly and fat. This is insane. It's as if they have been programmed to think like robots. None of them really believe they are pretty. Why is it like this and what can we do about it?

—Gretchen

What are women talking about *besides* diet and weight loss? What else are we encouraged to discuss? Every article I read, every story on the news, every piece of advice passed between friends seems to be aimed at some way to change and shift our bodies, to take away from our mass and strength and to make us small and amenable. Sure, there's nothing wrong with wanting to be the best version of you—but that is not the language I hear women using. I hear them berate themselves, belittle themselves, sabotage themselves—and sometimes they don't even know it. They are just repeating what is patterned for them in their lives. And sometimes we do know it but lack the courage to break free from it. Right now the pendulum needs to swing back to talking about life in terms of feelings, emotions, and experiences, not food, fat, or weight. Women should be able to talk and bond over a range of things—the least of which should be what they weigh.

Within our culture women are encouraged to pick apart their bodies. Entire industries are built around keeping us dissatisfied and separate from our glorious true selves. Speaking the Language of Fat is like an internalized form of slavery for women. The ideal, perfect image we strive to be is our master, and we are oppressed by the debasing thoughts, dialogue, and actions we take as we attempt to fulfill an image that doesn't really exist. It is not an attainable goal to be perfect, to be the best, the most loved, the nicest, the thinnest, the ultimate girl in the world. It's impossible. Those are fictional titles made up to sell us things, to keep us distracted from living full lives in the moment. There is no perfect woman.

How many minutes of your day are wasted in slavery to the Language of Fat?

Your brain is composed entirely of fat.

Walk Your Talk

Dear Jess,

I am so proud of my girlfriend, Shelly. She has survived a lot in her life, and her most recent triumph is over the bulimia that she started experiencing when she was just fourteen years old. For her it all started with "casual dieting" and then progressed into a full-blown eating disorder. I see her struggle daily with her weight and her food choices, but I also see her consistently decide to fight this disease. I never understood how much this body obsession could sweep into your life and almost steal it from you. She collapsed two years ago after a bad binge and ruptured her esophagus. She lost a lot of blood and we thought she was going to die. Now, two years later, she is a completely different person. And we both try our best to never utter another word in the Language of Fat again. I know her story may sound extreme, but it all started with her first diet and her first plunge into the irrational fears of being too fat.

—Michael

There are millions of women—and men—in this country whose lives are held hostage by the Language of Fat. The good news is, we are going to tackle this issue head-on, with truth, courage, levity, and a little action!

We cannot do everything at once, but we can do something at once. —Calvin Coolidge

---

In order to make a change in your everyday life, you need to be willing to walk your talk, to take action, to at least make the effort to make small steps. That can mean:

- listening more
- reaching out
- challenging your core beliefs
- standing up for yourself or others
- getting educated on a topic
- volunteering
- caring enough to take responsibility for yourself

Begin to build what I call a toolbox for life. In this toolbox you will gather new coping techniques, bits of knowledge, and practical, tangible tools for making changes in your life. Unfortunately, the toolbox doesn't come fully stocked. You have to build and collect these tools one by one. They come from your life.

TAKE ACTION

1. Recognize that the Language of Fat is not really about food, fat, or weight. Recognize that it is really all around you, in subtle and not so subtle ways.

2. Commit to keeping a notebook or journal to explore this issue. I find that writing things down really helps attain clarity, and it will be one of the primary tools to have in your toolbox.

3. Begin listening to the language around you and to the language you speak. Do you find yourself repeating a phrase or word that has a negative connotation? Begin to write down the most commonly repeated phrases.

4. For three days keep track of the number of times you use the words "fat" and "ugly." Also keep track of whom you say these words to. Do you say them to yourself? A boyfriend? A friend?

5. Begin to record some of the emotions that come up when you are speaking the Language of Fat. You don't have to be any more specific than writing down "pissed," "hungry," "hurt," whatever.

6. Decide if you are willing to take a deeper look into your own use of the Language of Fat. If so, get ready to recommit your willingness on a daily basis.

7. Go easy on yourself. It's just the beginning.

In the following chapters we'll start to translate some of the Language of Fat's most common phrases. You'll learn how to identify them, understand and translate them, and deny them their power.

Chapter Two

"Do I Look Fat in This?"

Most commonly heard:
In bedrooms, bathrooms, dorm rooms, boardrooms, living rooms, dressing rooms, and any other private or public place.

Translation(s):
Can mean any or all of the following, but is certainly not limited to:

"I need help!"

"I'm having a bad day!"

"I'm confused; I don't know how to ask for what I need!"

"I feel insecure!"

"I need you to pay attention to me!"

"I'm feeling unloved!"

If I Had a Dollar for Every Time Someone Asked Me That Question . . .

I was on the hunt for the perfect laptop. I had done as much online research as I could stomach before my head was aswirl with RAM and gigabytes, and I just wanted to get the purchase over with. I wandered into a Best Buy store a few hours before it closed. A young man named José approached me to help guide me through the computer department. In our conversation I told him that I was only going to be using this laptop to write a book called *Do I Look Fat in This?* José looked at me, made clear eye contact, and broke into a huge smile. "Why are you smiling like that?" I asked. "Has someone asked you that question before?"

José kept smiling, and then the smile turned into laughter. Uncontrollable laughter. With a little relief thrown in. Then he reached into his back pocket and pulled out his wallet.

"Look at this. This is a picture of my girl. Her name is Lisa. Does she look fat?"

He handed me the photograph. Standing front and center, with a hand on her hip and a faraway look in her eyes, was Lisa. She was a beautiful and very healthy-looking young woman.

"She asks me every single second of the day whether she's fat. It kills me. Look at her. She is so beautiful and I love her so much. And she just doesn't see it. I have no idea what to say to her," José told me.

As we talked, some of his colleagues, all male, gathered around us and pulled out pictures of their girlfriends. They were so aware, so concerned, so honestly baffled as to how it had gotten so bad that body loathing had crept into the lives of the women they loved and cared for. It was beyond humbling. It was fascinating to watch. They absorbed the information and asked incredibly insightful questions.

- **TONY:** "So when she asks if she's fat, I should just ask her to explain what she means, right? But what if she gets all defensive? What do I say then? Just keep at it, right? Like tough love but not so tough. More love, right?"

- **MIKE:** "Okay, so do you think that when my girlfriend is feeling bad about herself and goes out and spends hundreds of dollars on name-brand things that she thinks will make her feel better, that is like her Language of Fat, just taking it out in the material world, right? She tries to feel good by buying things!"

- **CJ:** "And when I tell her she's beautiful, she may not hear it, right? Even though I really mean it? So I should also talk about her inside things, too, so she feels that I respect her for who she is and not just her looks, right?"

- **JOSÉ** brought it to a close: "But, Jessica, my girl is only eighteen, and she should be focusing on things like going to college or getting a job or at least loving her life, right? Instead, she is focused on how many calories are in her salad. She is not even living a life right now. She is just waiting to love herself. That's kind of sad, isn't it?"

It was ten minutes till closing. Of course, I bought the laptop from José, and as I was leaving, he said to me, "I'm gonna talk to my girlfriend later and teach her about the Language of Fat." He was determined. This young man had a new education about body image and a new challenge. I knew he had it in him to make a difference.

> *We have women in the military, but they*
> *don't put us in the front lines. They*
> *don't know if we can fight, if we can*
> *kill. I think we can. All the general*
> *has to do is walk over to the women*
> *and say, "You see the enemy over*
> *there? They say you look fat*
> *in those uniforms."*
> —Elayne Boosler

He's Listening

Considering the interaction with José at Best Buy, I am not surprised that most of the e-mails I receive from men are about how to answer the question, "Do I look fat in this?" These men, confused, baffled, on-their-knees-and-ready-to-trade-their-prized-possessions-for-the-right-answer-to-this-question men, seem willing to do whatever it takes to have their girlfriends, sisters, or wives return from the body-image snatchers that have abducted them. The men in our lives have learned to adapt to the language we speak about our bodies, sometimes trying to get ahead of it, fix it, or solve it, and most of the time trying to avoid it.

Dear Jess,
    I swear my girlfriend asks me if she looks fat, like, one hundred times a day, and I find it boring! Really. Please help me. My girlfriend thinks she is fat and then doesn't believe me

when I tell her she is not. So I have just
stopped talking to her about it. I have stopped
trying to even answer this question, which is
just driving her crazy. So please tell me the
right response to the question, "Do I look fat
in this?"

—Peter

Have you ever really thought about how annoying you
can sound when you speak this language? It's not only boring to hear someone you adore berate themselves, but it's
also pretty frustrating to watch them self-destruct a hundred times a day and not feel like their partner is helping
them.

The most common mistake made in trying to answer
this question logically is forgetting that there is no logic in
the Language of Fat. If it were logical and rational, you
wouldn't be spending your lives sucking, tucking, nipping,
plucking, and worrying yourselves into heightened states of
anxiety over the size of your thighs or the shape of your
arms.

The first response you are conditioned to give when you
hear someone ask if they look fat is to say . . . all together
now . . .

"No!"

This is just one of the zillion Band-Aids you try to apply,
Band-Aids that are really just covering up a gaping wound.
The person asking this question doesn't even hear your
answer. She's on to the next body-hating thought.

There are typically ten different ways that a person can respond to the question "Do I look fat in this?"

1. **The Naysayer:** Always answers this question with "No." Firmly, clearly; never wavers from those two little letters.

2. **The Deer in Headlights:** This person knows that an oncoming collision is unavoidable; fear grips them, and they stay frozen, not sure what to say and how to react.

3. **The Indignant Naysayer:** Tries to emphatically express what a ridiculous question this is by raising his or her voice. "No, no, no, no, no, you are *not* fat! No way, not at all. No, no, no!"

4. **The Enabler:** Usually answers, "It's okay, honey, I'm a little chubby too. Let's go on a diet together, tomorrow."

5. **The Truth Speaker:** Dares to answer this question with an honest opinion. "You know, actually, that shirt is not flattering, and it does make you look a little wide."

6. **The Hearing Impaired:** A relative of the Deer in Headlights, this person usually pretends that he or she didn't hear the question. Not even if you are standing right in front of them. It's like they just suddenly went deaf.

7. **The Self-Flagellator:** Answers the question by focusing instead on his or her own flaws. "You think you're fat? Look at me! I'm a tub of lard. I'm beyond help. I am as big as a cruise ship; I should invite passengers on board my body and set sail!"

8. **The Codependent:** Immediately gets involved in helping the questioner find a better outfit.

9. **The Insulter:** Usually reserved for those who are fed up with this question, so they like to screw with the mind of the questioner and say things like, "Yes, you are fat. Can we go to the movies now?"

10. **The Overkiller:** This person is so wounded by hearing this question that he or she goes into overload with the self-help crap. "You are *more* than your body, you are the light embodied in the flesh, you are my reason to live, so how can you say that?"

He Said, She Said

In speaking with women, I have learned that they sometimes feel that if they act insecure, men will come to the rescue and pay attention and offer validation. They're fishing for compliments: "I hate my body, and you're going to fix it."

I suggest to men that they state up front that they aren't going to play that game. His goal is to not get sucked in. No matter what. No matter if she pouts, cries, stomps her foot, or tries to manipulate the conversation to make it about how much he doesn't care about her (all tactics women have admitted using in the past).

Now granted, I know that some men are not as comfortable with discussing emotions, but you know what? Get over it. This script and the following exercises are about delving deeper into the relationship you have. I recommend beginning the communication with a clear boundary.

Beginning the Translation

Her: *Babe? Do I look fat in this?*

Him: *I'm not doing this with you. What are you feeling right now?*

Her: *What do you mean? I just want to know if these pants make my legs look big. Can you just tell me, please?*

Him: *No. I will talk about what you're feeling, but not about your thighs. What can I do for you? How can I help?*

So far, this is designed to be merely a catalyst for further discussion. I guarantee that the conversation will take a dramatic turn, and that is why the script gets cut off so abruptly. There is no such thing as a touchy-feely quick fix. This tactic and this script are not for the faint of heart. You could discover that your partner is feeling some pretty deep stuff. Body-loathing is something that runs deeper than you anticipate. These kinds of exercises are for the strong of will and for those who share a determination to never hear their loved ones utter these words again. You have to be bold in your reversal of this language. And, quite frankly, you have to try something different in order to change. *You both must take a risk.*

You may not initially be aware of how your questioning makes your partner feel. But you have to take responsibility when asking this question, and you have to dig a little deeper.

Continuing the Translation

Her: *Babe? Do I look fat in this?*
Him: *What are you feeling right now?*

Women, please note: Before ripping off his head and running into the other room in response to his asking you this deeper question, take five really deep breaths. Step away from the mirror. Close your eyes. Take five more really deep breaths.

Him: *Honey? What is going on?*
Her: *You know what? I'm not sure what I'm feeling. Right now I think I'm feeling anxious. [Or insert other appropriate emotion here: angry, sad, excited, nervous, rushed, forced, disconnected, in need of a hug . . .]*

Remember . . .

Nothing else needs to be figured out in this moment. You don't have to apologize for speaking the Language of Fat. You just have to move on and continue to feel. That is it. Change your energy. Make a new decision. Decide to no longer go down that road. Communicate, and if you can't find the right words, at least recognize that it is not your breasts' or belly's fault. Take yourself out of the situation and keep it moving.

Take It Slow

You have choices. You can choose how you're going to treat yourself and your body. And if you have established a habit of mutilating and humiliating yourself in front of people you love by asking if you look fat, then it is going to take a concerted effort to change. Will you do it perfectly right away? No. Will it be perfect the first ten times? Probably not. But try to enjoy the process along the way. At least you won't be talking about your fat butt anymore. Well, at least not at that moment.

You must understand the native tongue and all the colloquialisms in order to master a language. And questions like "Do I look fat in this?" are a part of a special language. These suggestions may not always fix the immediate problem, but I do guarantee that after a few rounds of trying on these new responses, you will discover something much richer about yourself and your loved one.

> *Do you love yourself enough to ask for what you need? —Rusty Berkus*

The "But" Factor

Dear Jess,

My sister and I are roommates. She has everything going for her. She is bright, funny, supersmart, and a very good friend. But no matter what, before she leaves the house, she asks me if she looks fat. It's automatic—just like hello or good-bye. Nothing I say makes her feel better, so I just laugh it off or brush it

off. She always seems to leave the house not
feeling good about herself. I'm not even sure
she realizes just how many times she asks me
this question.

—Patrice

I can't tell you how many times I have heard someone say
about a woman in their life, "She is funny, smart, beautiful,
kind, loving, *but . . .*" and then go on to talk about how that
person doesn't see it, or feel it, or that she just isn't happy
with her life. You resign yourself to expect this from other
women. What you fail to recognize is that this is not normal,
and left unchallenged, this language continues to destroy the
lives of your incredibly funny, smart, and beautiful sisters.

Why does the person in your life who matters most to
you, your blood and best friend, not realize how much she is
loved? Why is it that she can be so loving and kind to everyone but herself? The hardest thing to recognize is that you
can't love your sisters into loving themselves. They have to
choose it. They have to recognize that they are worth more
than what the Language of Fat assigns them.

"Fat chance" and "slim chance"
mean the same thing.

Dig a Little Deeper

I know most people think that when a girl or woman asks if
she looks fat, she is just looking for an easy compliment. Most
people perceive that question to be only a manipulative tool
to get someone's attention.

And the truth is, they are right. To some degree. When a person asks, "Do I look fat in this?" they want you to pay attention to them. To acknowledge them. To validate them. But they also want something more. They are longing for something they don't even know how to ask for.

In the past, every time I used those words, I was looking for someone to show me that I was deserving, that I was lovable, that I was allowed to be who I am. "Fat" meant something else. It didn't mean overweight. It meant ostracized. Different. Ignored. Unloved. Isolated.

This question is usually not an invitation for conversation, but the trick is to make it one. Make it about something deeper—because it is. And don't be afraid of where it goes. It may get more emotional (yes, I mean crying and deep feelings) before it gets better.

It's Not Just for Girls

Dear Jess,

My husband, Paul, and I have been married for three years. He has always been a little overweight, but I find it cute. Me, I can eat anything I want and I am the same size as I was in high school. I couldn't really care less about fashion and clothing and how I dress. But my husband is becoming obsessed with the way he looks. He recently lost ten pounds on a crash diet where he drank most of his meals, and yesterday, in his office, I found a stack of articles on how to lose weight and dress to make yourself look slimmer. You would think that those came from my women's magazines, but they didn't—they were in his men's magazines, and you would die if you saw some of these titles: "Chase Away the Flab in Seven Days" and "Tone Up or Lose Her!" I couldn't believe it. Has it gotten that bad for men? He asks me if he looks fat in his clothes. You never hear this from a man, really. He is acting like a woman. What on earth do I say to him?

—Linda

Men, too, can speak in the code of body hatred because they are not able to access yet what they really want to express. The Language of Fat is really about emotions, feelings, and experiences not being fully expressed. What was once perceived as a woman's issue is no longer just that. This language is now an equal opportunity offender, impacting all races, classes, and genders.

And, of course, men experience self-consciousness and low self-esteem, because they're also being marketed to and receiving the same messages that women have been getting for decades. Men are definitely being targeted as a part of the mammoth diet and health industry that capitalizes on our fears and insecurities about our bodies.

One out of five men would trade three to five years of [his] life to achieve [his] goal body weight. —Rader Programs

Watch how you speak about your body around your partner. Do you encourage him when he is dieting, and are you harsh on him when he has "failed" or "slipped"? Do you speak the Language of Fat with him? If you are becoming more concerned because your husband's or boyfriend's daily life seems to be interrupted by his obsession with losing weight, then I suggest you sit down with him and begin talking. Try not to fall into gender stereotypes on this one. Many men stay secretive and shameful because they don't think they should be having these feelings. Remember, we are all human in the end. No one is immune from the Language of Fat. Not even our husbands, brothers, boyfriends, sons, and male best friends.

It Starts at Birth

The Language of Fat is a learned language. We were not born with the belief system that tells us that we are flawed or in need of fixing; that we are not worth our existence in the world, not worth our happiness, unless we create a surface exterior or possess material goods that make us worthy. That is a diseased set of ideas that we accumulate as we grow up—we mimic what we learn at home and copy what we see in our peer circles. Most of all, we internalize these messages because they are everywhere.

When you first started out, you were like a blank slate of body love. Have you ever seen babies sit around commiserating over their chubby thighs? Hell, no! They are proud of their flesh; they wobble in their fullness, exposing their round bellies, meaty arms, and triple chins. To babies and children, bodies are triumphant, useful, meaningful, and important parts of how they express themselves in the world.

I just spent some time with a family whose four-year-old twin girls were caught trying to walk on the family treadmill. When asked what they were doing, the girls said they had "big butts" and had to walk them off! This is shocking, and it should be. But it just illustrates how this language of self-destruction and distraction is getting passed down to our children.

You may not even be aware of who is listening when you speak this language. If you have younger siblings or take care of young children or mentor youth groups, or even when you are out in public spaces, there are young ears within range.

The Responsibility Is Yours

I was amazed during a recent visit to the food court at the mall—and it wasn't because there is always the same man serving teriyaki chicken samples at every food court across America. It was because in the line for the lemonade/slushy/frozen yogurt stand, I overheard this conversation among three girls who couldn't have been older than twelve or thirteen:

Girl No. 1: *How many calories do you think are in a nonfat frozen yogurt?*

Girl No. 2: *I don't know, but probably more than I can have today. I am already over my limit by, like, a million.*

Girl No. 3: *I wonder if they can just, like, put some ice in the cup for me. I'm just*

> *gonna chew on the ice. That way I have,*
> *like, zero calories and my mouth is*
> *busy doing something!*

These girls were not even through puberty yet! Restriction and starvation are normalized for young girls. Go into any school cafeteria, and it is no surprise at all to see girl after girl sitting with a Diet Coke and a bunch of untouched carrot sticks. No one questions her. No one challenges her. No one even worries about her, really. You are too busy counting your own calories.

You have a responsibility to speak a language that upholds the vision of healthy body image for generations to come.

He who trims himself to suit everyone will soon whittle himself away. —Raymond Hull

---

It's Not Normal

Here's the question to ask yourself at this point: How much of your day is spent focusing on your weight, your food intake, what you "should" be eating, how much you "need" to be exercising, what your life "will" look like when you have it under "control"? If more than one percent of your day is spent on these thoughts, then think about what else you are missing out on. From now on when you hear the question "Do I look fat in this?" you will have a choice as to how to respond. And you'll know to pause and think when you feel yourself beginning to ask it. No matter what, remember that this question is not what it seems. It is code. It is a cry for help. It is not "normal." And it is not harmless.

TAKE ACTION

1. Remember that "Do I look fat?" is not just a question. It's a cry for help. It is a basic phrase in the Language of Fat. This is like speaking a foreign language; you must learn to translate it and decode it. This will take time.

2. Record in your journal or notebook how many times during the day you or someone else asks the question "Do I look fat in this?" Start by recording for one day, then try to monitor one week, and work up to one month.

3. Try to pin down what you feel when you hear this question. Also make note of where you were when you heard it. What was going on?

4. Be careful of how you speak about your body and others' in front of children. Do your best to always focus on inner qualities (courage, humor, kindness) when engaging with young people.

5. This question can present an opportunity for you to make a new choice about how to respond to it. Remember, however, that you may not always get the response you desire the first time you try.

6. Continue to look beyond this question for the meaning behind it.

7. To decode this language you must be willing to take a risk. Be the change you wish to see in the world!

Chapter Three

"I Feel Fat!"

Most commonly heard:
Being uttered by me, you, all of our friends, strangers, men, and people we'd never fathom would say this sentence.

Translation(s):
Can mean any of the following, but is not limited to:
"I feel lonely, scared, isolated, unattractive, unprepared, angry, excited, intimidated, overwhelmed, insecure, full, rejected, or even happy!"

What Are You Really Saying?

It's not what you think. Really. I know we all say it; heck, it's the battle cry for most women in this country. We could just go ahead and replace all formal greetings with "I feel fat," and we would get the same response: welcome smiles, knowing glances, and deep bonding. Just imagine. You arrive at work, and instead of saying hello to a coworker, you have the following conversation:

You: *Do you feel fat today?*
Coworker: *Oh yes, I feel fat.*
You: *Right, me too, I feel soooo fat.*
Coworker: *Exactly. Really, really fat!*

Sometimes that's what it sounds like when we talk with each other. We bypass any sort of real connecting in favor of the lowest common denominator between women—body-loathing. It's simple, it's understandable (kind of), and it makes us all feel better. When our girlfriends, best friends, or even strangers talk about how fat they feel, we feel more comfortable with how fat we feel, and it all becomes one giant body-loathing, fat-feeling party. But it's the most misunderstood phrase in the English language.

Fat Is Not a Feeling

It's not. It is not an emotion. Pain, anger, joy, sadness—those are emotions. Fat has just become a catchall phrase we assign to the emotions that we are at a loss to describe. Our vocabulary has become dramatically simplified with regard to this exchange. We are so used to including the word "fat" as a reliable emotion. And the reason it works is that all women think they understand what it means to *feel* fat.

On some level it means that we feel uncomfortable with who we are in that moment. We feel insecure, fragile, frustrated with our own progress or lack of discipline, and we become chopped down by this word. That, therefore, makes us more relatable and identifiable to the person we are speaking with. For instance, that bizarre conversation with your coworker would never go like this:

You: *Hi, how are you today?*
Coworker: *Well, I feel fat.*

You: *Come on, we all know fat is not a*
             feeling. What are you really
             feeling?

Coworker: *I'm feeling depressed today because*
             my boyfriend and I have been broken up
             for about two weeks, and I feel like
             I've made a terrible mistake leaving
             him, but I'm too stubborn to call him
             and tell him that.

You: *Ah, that makes perfect sense. I've been*
             there too.

It sounds a little cheesy, but think about it. This conversation at least had a trace of honesty in it, didn't it? True emotions. And it might not be your job to stick around and fix someone's feelings of being depressed. But what a relief it would be to actually just tell the truth to each other.

Now, I know that there are such things as social graces and self-defense mechanisms and polite gestures between acquaintances. And I also know that most days we don't want to be bothered with what the other person is *truly* feeling, or share how we feel. We try to stay on the surface. But until someone (you) decides to discard the Language of Fat in their (your) life, communication will stay on the surface, separated and unsupported. So that is the challenge I offer with "I feel fat." How far are you willing to go to exchange the catchall phrase for an interaction that is more honest about your emotions?

But Fat *Feels* Like a Feeling . . .

Dear Jess,

Fat *is* a feeling. I *do* feel fat. It's a real feeling for me. I can feel my belly hang over my pants, especially when I eat too much, and it disgusts me. I hate feeling like this. So this isn't a made-up feeling, and when I say "I feel fat," I really mean it!

I always overeat! I can't stop. Appetizer, main course, dessert, I eat everything. Even when I say I am going to have discipline and stop, I don't. So at the end of the meal, I am bloated, I feel fat. I can literally feel my stomach hang over my pants, and it is embarrassing and gross. I feel fat pretty much after every time I eat something. I have no control. So when you say that feeling fat really means you are feeling something else, I don't get it. Because what I am feeling is indulgent and *fat*!

—Claudia

I know that the feeling of being stuffed and full can feel really bad. It can feel like we have overindulged, which also means we have disregarded our inner guide that told us to stop eating or to make different food choices. It feels terrible to not honor ourselves, to push ourselves to the limit.

Claudia used the word "indulgent" alongside the word "fat." This is exactly what I mean when I say that "I feel fat" also means something else. In this case the indulgence can be Claudia's perception that she's gone beyond her self-imposed limits (something we can all relate to!). There are always other feelings floating around. Here are some that I glimpsed in Claudia's e-mail: indulgent, not in control, angry, disappointed, frustrated, fed up, dissatisfied, and fearful.

Even though we associate a physical feeling with the word, whether that is bloating, nausea, or indigestion, there is still a more complicated emotion lurking at the root. For Claudia the fat feeling wasn't a feeling at all, but rather a catchall word to describe those other emotions. Sometimes the word "fat" seems to be more easily understood than the actual feelings are. Get it?

I have been on a diet for two weeks and all I've lost is fourteen days. —Totie Fields

---

Decoding "I feel fat" is hard because we make an automatic association between fat and food. The words have become synonymous in our dieting language, in our marketing language, and in the body-loathing language women share. Yet it is crucial that we understand that fat isn't a real feeling, especially when we're around food.

We have been taught to put food into two broad categories: good and bad. And usually we associate our emotions with the kind of food we think we're eating. For instance, we feel good when we eat foods like salads and fruits. And we feel bad about ourselves for eating bad foods like cookies and chips. This duality is at the heart of disordered eating and it is mucking up our understanding of our true emotions, regardless of what we are putting in our mouths. It's important to recognize that we are more than what we are eating—it is first about what's eating us.

Pass the Hors d'Oeuvres, Please

Everyone always hangs around the kitchen at parties. There can be a zillion square feet of beautiful house to mingle in, but most people gravitate to the kitchen. And there, people are magnetically drawn to the food platters where, once the group eating rules are established (no double dipping), enormous amounts of time are spent discussing one or more of the following:

1. How good the food is.
2. How fattening the food is.
3. How good and fattening the food is.
4. What foods we shouldn't eat.
5. Why we have to go ahead and eat those foods anyway.
6. What diets everyone's been on lately.
7. What new diet has been featured on TV.
8. What new diet you will start after this party (probably on Monday).
9. How good the food is.

Stop talking for a second at the next party you attend and just listen to some conversations around you. Count how many times the words "fat" or "diet" come up in the conversation, especially if you are in the kitchen. We do it unconsciously, and it may seem really innocuous, but consider the idea that every time you utter a sentence like "I feel fat" you are robbing yourself of an experience of closeness and self-reliance.

Try writing emotion as two separate words:
E-motion. E = energy. Energy in motion.
It must move through your body in order
to be felt fully. —Dr. Steve Nenninger

There was a time in my life when "I feel fat!" fell out of my mouth so often that no one even noticed that I was in a tremendous amount of pain. All of my female friendships had some sort of body-hating component to them. To be quite fair, I'm not sure we even knew how much we were hurting. We felt like we were being girls, talking about girl things. Food, fat, weight. You know, the important stuff. (Insert sarcasm here.)

It wasn't until I began paying attention to this language that I started to realize how much was missing from my female connections. I noticed just how hard it was to stay intimate with my girlfriends if I wasn't body-loathing beside them. And even if I was out with my more evolved women friends who were also trying to take note of the words they chose, the world at large was still speaking this language.

Dear Jess,

I always feel fat when I hang around this one particular friend of mine, who is incredibly thin and beautiful. She doesn't talk about her weight at all, but people around her always ask her how she stays so thin. I immediately think that they must think I am *huge*, and then I do this disturbed dance in my head where I start to beat myself up. What can I do to change this?
—Brooke

This kind of thing happens all the time. You are out with your good girlfriend, enjoying yourself, minding your own business, and someone asks an intimate and personal question about weight and body size. It never ceases to amaze me that people actually feel they have the right to comment on someone else's body. Whose business is it how or why someone is thin, fat, tall, short, blond, or brunette?

Come up with a sassy way to back someone off when they ask these questions. If the person is a stranger, just say, "That question is inappropriate and none of your business." Leave it at that. Simple and clear. And try your best to stay focused on what matters . . . your friendship!

There isn't much you can do about someone else's ignorance and lack of understanding. What you can control is whether you automatically associate this experience with feeling fat. I can understand frustrated, left out, judged, angry, violated, imposed on, fed up, and insecure. But I don't see where fat fits into this equation. This is not some contest between you and your friend.

Walk Your Talk

Dear Jess,

For as long as I can recall, I have wanted to disappear. To just become so small and insignificant that people wouldn't notice my size or my existence at all. I was naturally thin to begin with, which made it harder for anyone in my family to realize that I had an eating disorder, because they just expected me to be thin. And since everyone in this world wants to be thin, no one thought to ask me any deeper questions or challenge how small my body was becoming.

About a year into my recovery, I was in this bathroom with all of my sorority sisters and I heard one of them say, "God, I feel so fat." And another answered, "Yeah, I wish I could just be anorexic for the night because I feel so huge right now." I know they didn't really realize what they were saying, and I debated interrupting them until their conversation came my way. One of the girls said, "God, Patty, I would give anything to be as skinny as you are. I bet you never feel fat!"

Then I had no choice but to speak up. I told her that she was really off base, because I had in fact been anorexic, and not just for one night but for almost four years, and that I wouldn't wish for anyone to be as "skinny" as I was because I almost lost my life, wasting away. And with regard to never feeling fat—*ha!*—I told her that the feeling of being too fat was a sick thought that crept into my mind every second of the day! I told her that anorexia is not an adjective, it is a disease, and that she should choose her words more carefully next time—just because people are thin doesn't mean they are also happy with their bodies! I know it may have come off a little harsh, but I get so sick of hearing people make assumptions about thin women too.

—Patricia

Anorexia is not an adjective. It is not a privilege, a gift, or a blessing. It is a life-threatening disease that kills thousands of women. In our absentminded pursuit of fashionable thinness, we lose sight of the reality of this issue. This kind of offhand, toxic conversation can actually be quite effective in hurting someone's feelings and perpetuating stereotypes.

> **Believe it or not, people who are naturally thin also have a hard time navigating the Language of Fat in our society. They, too, are seen not as full human beings, but as dress sizes.**

I understand that we have been brainwashed to believe a sentence like "I feel fat" is no big deal. We think it so often, speak it so often, and hear it so often that it may even feel rebellious to challenge the use of this language in our lives. We must begin to exchange destructive thoughts and language for more proactive thoughts and empowering words.

Feed Your Mind
Top Five Translations for "I Feel Fat!"

1. *I feel scared.*

   Fear can come in many scenarios. Blind dates, job interviews, public performances, even falling in love. When we feel scared, we often just move that feeling down to our thighs, hips, butt, or anywhere that seems more controllable.

2. *I feel angry.*

   There is nothing like good ol' rage to make us feel like we are taking up too much space. Oftentimes our anger, whether directed inside or out, is so scary to feel that we confuse that intensity with weight gain. Silly us. We have to become more comfortable feeling the anger and quit blaming it on our bloated bellies or chafing upper arms.

3. *I feel excited.*

Yes, you can have a *good* feeling and somehow equate it with feeling fat. Why? Well, because if you don't think you're worthy of this emotion, it's easy to turn this uncomfortable (but good) feeling into a sense of being out of control. And for some reason, in the Language of Fat, feeling out of control equals feeling fat.

4. *I feel sad.*

As with anger, we are often afraid of the intense feelings of sadness, so it is much easier to focus instead on what we are eating or not eating or how much we weigh. Sometimes sadness feels heavy. We just have to let ourselves feel the weight of this emotion (pun intended).

5. *I feel unworthy.*

At the heart of feeling unworthy is the sense of being not good enough, undeserving, insecure, or overwhelmed. This can creep up when you're surrounded by hurtful media imagery, destructive friendships, or other unhealthy triggers.

We move from feeling unworthy to feeling fat because it is much more acceptable for us to talk about our bodies than to talk about our innermost thoughts and fears.

Choose Your Weapon

In social settings most of the awkward silence that follows a statement like "I feel fat" can be attributed to everyone's absolute uncertainty of how to respond.

There can be a lot of humor in discussing body image, and sometimes we just want to be left alone to laugh at our foibles. For many of us our friendships and bonding have taken place while joking about our big butts or saddlebags, so when someone interjects with therapeutic sincerity, it can go over like a fart in church. My suggestion is to take each scenario as it comes and be prepared for a few different kinds of interchanges. You can do any of the following:

1. IGNORE THE COMMENTS

This just isn't an option. Take action!

2. CHANGE THE SUBJECT

Scenario: When your friend or coworker mentions for the tenth time in one evening how gross she looks or how those last five pounds cling to her like saran wrap, you can simply try to move on to some other topic of conversation.

Pro: This is the most polite way out of an awkward moment. It may also be the most painless, but it doesn't stop your friend or coworker from starting up again after the new subject loses steam. It is the most common way people respond to this statement.

Con: You had better make sure that you are prepared

to really jump in there with your thoughts on the genocide in Sudan or the newest sale at Top Shop, because most of us love to dish about our physical shortcomings, and the attention is most likely going to swing back to your pal's fat ass. Let's face it, we just can't help ourselves.

3. THE BOLD CONFRONTATION

Scenario: When your friend or loved one continues to mumble under her breath, "Ugh, I feel so fat," etc., you can look her square in the eye and say, "I've had enough of this kind of talk. It is no longer welcome here!"

Pro: It is a very bold and clear way to intercept the body-loathing before it spreads like an airborne virus to the rest of the people around you.

Con: This isn't a freakin' Clint Eastwood movie. A body image showdown is not what most people crave. People hate confrontation, especially if you are with a group or about to draw guns at high noon.

4. THE GENTLE CONFRONTATION

Scenario: Your friend always greets you with a laundry list of everything that's wrong with her. You decide to tell her, "Look, it hurts me when you say those things about yourself. What else is really going on?"

Pro: This sort of confrontation addresses the issue head-on but keeps the statements focused on how you feel terrible hearing those things, not how your friend is terrible for saying those things.

Con: If you are dealing with a seasoned body hater, you may get some resistance and resentment for talking about how you feel, when she's feeling so shitty!

5. THE COMBO:
ASK QUESTIONS—BOLD AND GENTLE CONFRONTATIONS

Scenario: Some intense body loathers need a giant wake-up call.

```
Friend: I feel so fat!
You:    Why do you say things like that about
        yourself? What do you need from me right
        now? I hate it when you say that about
        yourself. I never know how to respond to
        you. It drives me nuts to hear you say
        things like that!
```

You could opt for a gentler confrontation.

```
Friend: I feel so fat!
You:    Fat is not a feeling. You know, I notice
        that you say that a lot, and it really
        hurts me when I hear you say that,
        because you're so important to me. How
        can I help you?
```

Trust your gut on this one. Use questions, boldness, or gentleness as you feel fit. The most important thing is that you do something.

Pro: This combo approach allows you to have many options in responding and can be infused with humor, grace, and kindness.

Con: Sometimes people aren't sure how to respond once more dialogue has been initiated. Remember, part of theproblem is that it feels more comfortable to berate yourself than to delve deeper. It may take some time and practice before you feel comfortable using the combo routine.

Get an Extreme Language Makeover
Language Exchange Guide

Instead of using the word "fat"—or any of the words in the Language of Fat—as your emotion, go through the replacement emotions and see if there is another that is a more accurate description of what you are feeling.

A Short Vocabulary of the Language of Fat

Pudgy	Nasty	Failure
Chubby	Dumb	Heinous
Tubby	Stupid	Hate
Round	Lazy	Monster
Large	Worthless	Horrible
Portly	Pig	Wicked
Flabby	Hopeless	Undeserving
Huge	Boring	Not good enough
Hefty	Pitiful	Unattractive
Thick	Loser	A lost cause
Big	Appalling	Idiotic
Chunky	Evil	Sinful
Stout	Imperfect	Broken
Ugly	Useless	Disgusting
Gross	Awful	Pathetic

Replacement Emotions for the Language of Fat

Angry	Unhappy	Empathetic
Sad	Wounded	Sympathetic
Happy	Hurt	Bold
Elated	Frustrated	Displeased
Overwhelmed	Joyous	Blessed
Excited	Disconnected	Grateful
Nervous	Discounted	Proud
Anxious	Bullied	Pleased
Scared	Unloved	Apologetic
Discarded	Remorseful	Alive
Ignored	Hopeful	Worthy
Isolated	Eager	Satisfied
Rejected	Inspired	Strong
Challenged	Unprepared	Prepared
Uncomfortable	Unsure	Encouraged

Response Phrases:
Some Suggestions for Ways to Respond to "I Feel Fat!"

"Fat is not a feeling!"

"You know, it hurts me to hear you say things like that about yourself."

"What is really going on with you?"

"Has anything happened?"

"What do you need?"

"What can I do?"

"I've realized lately that we spend a lot of time talking about our bodies, and I would love to talk about something else, please!"

"I really find self-loathing to be boring. Next subject, please!"

"Sorry, I just won't sit by while another amazing woman destroys herself or picks apart her body."

"Why do we always have to bond by hating our bodies?"

"Sorry, I just don't speak the Language of Fat!"

The vision must be followed by the venture.
It is not enough to stare up the steps—
we must also step up the stairs.
—Vance Havner

TAKE ACTION

1. Remember that *fat is not a feeling.*

2. Recognize that "I feel fat" is a catchall phrase for a much deeper emotion or circumstance.

3. Don't be afraid to ask deeper questions of yourself and others. Questions like "What else am I really feeling?" or "What just happened, before I felt fat?"

4. Refer to the Language Exchange Guide when you are stuck in the Language of Fat. Find other terms/phrases/emotions that will help you communicate what you really feel.

5. Be aware that even though you are trying to decode the Language of Fat, not everyone will be doing the same. Stay focused on your goals and your language and intentions.

6. Feel free to make additions and changes to the guide. Continue to change this guide as you amass more tools in your toolbox.

Chapter Four

"If I Were Thinner, He'd Love Me!"

Most commonly heard:
In remnants of bad advice, fashion magazines, and our twisted little heads.

Translation(s):
Can mean any of the following, but is not limited to:

"I can't control the way another person feels about me, so I will attempt to control the only thing I know, which is my body shape and size."

"I am living my life in a fantasy mode and not facing the fact that anyone worth being with will accept and love my body as is."

"I am putting all the blame for this relationship not working out on my thighs and stomach."

You Treat Your Body the Way You Treat Love

The way you treat your body is the way you treat your romantic relationships.

Are you punishing, demanding, unrealistic, unrelenting, even delusional? Or are you in denial, passive aggressive, hopeless? A common message to women is that you will be loved when you are thinner. And why wouldn't you think so? In every advertisement, commercial, TV show, and movie, only the thin, pretty girls get the guys. And in your everyday life this theory seems valid as you watch other women obsess about the shape of their physical beings, terrified of not being attractive to the opposite sex. Does your obsession about your body get in the way of forming loving, lasting relationships in your life? Does your body image impede or improve your romantic endeavors?

From the Mouths of Babes

I was eight when I learned how to suck in my stomach to appear thinner. I had a crush on Ryan, the smelliest boy in third grade. But at that time odor didn't matter as much as the way he wore his two different-colored sneakers and the way he made me laugh. Yes, I had a crush on the hygiene-impaired class clown. One day I was in the bathroom with two friends, Bethany and April, and they both began to pull up their shirts to reveal their flat tummies. Mine was a bit fleshier than those of my counterparts, although I wasn't aware that this was a bad thing. Not yet, anyway. I asked them what they were doing as they stood side by side in front of the mirror and took turns holding their breath and sucking in their stomachs so hard that you could practically see their kidneys. Then they would exhale and let out a lot of squealing and laughter. It seemed like a fun thing to do, for some reason, so I joined them.

"No, suck it in more, Jessie, make it flat." I kept sucking and sucking, and mine still didn't look like their tummies. My belly button made more of an oblong shape than the perfect circles the other two girls had. "If you don't suck it in, the boys won't like you," Bethany said.

"Really? Why not?" I responded.

"Because," Bethany said, "my mom told me that boys like girls with flat stomachs."

And so it was. The edict had been passed down from Bethany's mom, to Bethany, to me. It wasn't clear whether Bethany's mother realized she was planting the first seeds of intense self-scrutiny and a faulty value system in her child. But what was clear was that I had to have the flattest stomach ever—or else Ryan would never notice me.

The message that girls had to somehow shape and change their bodies to get a boy's attention carried me through into junior high when Tara, our school's most voluptuous and sexually advanced vixen, informed my group of friends that when you went to the beach with a group of guys, you were supposed to stand up as little as possible. "As soon as you lay your towel down, get on top of it and lay horizontal, so that all of your fat hangs to the back. You always look skinnier when you're lying down."

I remember asking for more clarification on the rules. "So you don't get up, ever?"

Tara, annoyed that I was challenging her worldly ways, snapped back, "Don't get up. Ever. Just lie there and suck it in."

I still had my doubts: "What if you have to go to the bathroom?"

"Well, you can get up if you need to go to the bathroom, but otherwise you should be lying down so the boys can't see what you look like in your bathing suit."

As I advanced through the years, I realized that seeing me in my bathing suit was exactly what boys wanted and that lying down the entire time you were at the beach was kind of lame and a great way to get a sunburn. So the confusion set in early on. Do I hide my body in order to attract a guy? Then, once he's attracted, do I let him see my body? And what about how I feel about my body along the way?

Through high school and beyond I tormented myself with bizarre and extreme diets, all in an effort to "finally" lose some weight and get a boyfriend! By this stage in my life my priorities were clear: lose weight, get a boyfriend, be envied by everyone around me, lose more weight, keep the boyfriend, and never gain weight again.

As I grew older, my fears moved from what he would think if he saw me in a bathing suit to what I would do if, when we were making out, he tried to touch my stomach. Or wanted to have sex with the lights on. Or worse, what if he saw me naked, with the lights on, after he touched my stomach, while we were making out and having sex?

Our Bodies, Ourselves

I have spent years blaming my body for my unfulfilled romantic relationships. And the more punitive and punishing I got toward my body, the more that energy would show up in my relationships. In fact, I can correlate the men I have dated with the diets I've been on.

- **The Grapefruit Diet:** While ingesting at least eight whole grapefruits a day, I was also attracted to bitter and boring Roger, who took to criticizing the grammar in my romantic e-mails to him. He wasn't a lot of fun. He was angry at the world and reminded me that I, too, was angry—for letting citrus rule my life. I lasted for about eleven days on the Grapefruit Diet and put up with Roger's human spell-check act for about two weeks.

- **The Low-Carb Diet:** I gave up everything I enjoyed in my life: bagels, chips, and generous lovers. The guy I dated during the low-carb craze was from Italy, and while his entire country was a carb addict's dream, Sebastian was not mine. While I restricted carbs from ever entering my mouth, Sebastian was equally as restrictive in his feelings toward me.

- **The High-Protein Diet:** I met Carl at the gym, and we managed to flirt mercilessly in between our protein shakes and power push-ups. He was big and beefy, like the meals I was forcing myself to eat, but there was no substance to him. He didn't understand my quest for a career, and I didn't understand how he could be so . . . stupid.

- **The Raw-Foods Diet:** Paul was a smelly, dirty hippy I met in a raw foods cooking class. We were soaking our beans together when he asked me out. Of course we couldn't go out anywhere to eat, so we ended up staying in and making our own nut cheese at his place. And if this sounds equal parts boring and disturbing to you, it also sums up my relationship with Paul, in a nut(cheese)shell.

- **The Juice Fast:** Enough said. I didn't date anyone during this period because I was too consumed with squeezing the juice out of everything I wanted to eat. That takes time and energy and discipline, and after ingesting five liquid meals a day, who had time to date?

> The crazy bottom line is that how I treated myself during these diets manifested itself in all of my romantic relationships. I didn't have much to offer as a self-obsessed, calorie-counting gym addict who cared more about how my butt looked in a pair of jeans than I did about communicating openly and honestly with my partner. I was all about the "get," not the "gotten." I had no idea who to be in my relationships because all of my focus was in the wrong place.

A woman watches her body uneasily, as though it were an unreliable ally in the battle for love. —Leonard Cohen

---

It's All Control

The hardest thing to accept in life is that you cannot control anyone else. No matter how hard you try, you can't make someone like you or love you without their desire to do so. You can't control whether they call you back, treat you well, or tell you the truth. I know there are other theories out there saying that we can manipulate, contort, contrive, and scheme in our relationships, but in my experience you cannot control another person, ever.

That poses a problem when you aren't getting what you need or want. The tendency is to do one of two things: Blame the other person or blame yourself. Seems logical. But remember, we're talking about the Language of Fat, and the Language of Fat is comprised of a bunch of feelings, thoughts, and actions, and a belief system that does not serve you in the reality of your life. Those who have been speaking the Language of Fat for some time will choose to break down failed or stalled or problematic relationships into the following equations:

Problem in a Relationship = It Was My Fault
Not Getting the Love I Desire = I Am Not Worthy
Being Rejected in a Relationship = I Deserved It

Sound familiar? It may not always be such an obvious equation in your mind, but, as a woman brought up in this world, somewhere deep inside you feel like you should have control over the outcome of your relationships. Well, that just ain't the way it's done. There are actually three people in every relationship. You, your partner, and the couple you are together. In your individual lives you will have formed thoughts and opinions about your selves, your worth, and your bodies. What you bring together as a couple is the sum total of your individual views. It is an error to believe that another person can fix you, heal you, or love you enough for you to love yourself.

I can't count how many times over the years I have sat with crying, enraged women who are recounting the failures and frustrations of their relationships, which they seem to think stem from the way they look. The truth is, you can choose to spend your time believing it is the size of your hips that helps your relationships, or you can really look at who you are attracting and allowing into your life. It hurts to be rejected, to be disappointed. But it doesn't hurt nearly as much as burying that feeling, hiding it, and dieting over it.

When you're ready to really delve into the fact that how you treat your body is how you treat your relationships, you'll discover a bounty of self-knowledge, relief, and inspiration to take action. I can't promise it won't be hard and emotional, but I can promise that you will be a stronger person for it.

> *Love is or it ain't. Thin love ain't love at all!* —Toni Morrison

Looking for Love in All the Wrong Places

I was in a relationship for the better part of my teens and twenties. And when I found myself single at twenty-six, I also discovered the bar scene for the first time. The bizarre rituals of painting your face, slithering into tight, sexy clothing, and praying to God you hooked up with a stranger were a new and delicious world to me. Each bar experience was like a gambling game of bluffing, risking, upping, and bluffing some more. Your currency was your body and your looks. If you pretended that anything else mattered, well, you were just dumb or in denial.

Be in Your Skin

If the bar scene isn't your bag (after a few visits, it wasn't mine), then there is always the Internet. For a while Internet dating had the unfortunate stigma of seeming creepy and desperate. But these days anyone who has gone surfing for their partner online through one of those super-sassy sites will tell you that it can be a ton of fun to look for love online.

With online dating, however, you can play all sorts of body-image games, because it is initially a very visual process. First of all, you are often asked to describe your body type. Then you discover that most people see their body shape and size to be different from what it really is. We call this the "funhouse mirror" effect. What you see is never really what you get. Men lie. Women lie. And everyone knows they do it, as though people won't eventually discover that you aren't six feet tall or that you don't have a "slender and toned" body. Come on. He will eventually see your body and know what you look like. Don't pretend that you don't have the body you have. Be in your skin. It is better to be extremely honest when it comes to accurately describing your body type, because who wants to start out a relationship with a lie? Same goes for age, height, and occupation. Tell the truth. This is not the time to invent a new identity.

There have been so many times I have played Gumby, trying to bend, stretch, and fold myself into being with someone who just wasn't a complete match. The temptation to settle for something because you don't feel you will get the whole package is also tied into our self-esteem and self-worth. You deserve to have the real deal. Someone who loves you, respects you, enjoys similar things, challenges you, inspires you, adores you, and likes you!

> *Always be a first-rate version of yourself, not a second-rate version of someone else. —Judy Garland*

Break the Pattern

Dear Jess,

I have tried *everything* to meet a great guy. I have done online dating, blind dates, even speed dating. Each guy I meet seems promising. He takes my number, promises to call, and then doesn't. I feel rejected and unattractive. Every time this happens, I find myself in my kitchen bingeing on something sweet. Then I feel guilty and start a new diet the next morning (which I only stay on till the next date).

Anyway, I just feel like if I could get my eating under control, then I might be able to attract the right guy. Any thoughts?

—Marianne

It hurts to be rejected. It destroys your self-confidence. It offers you no real reason sometimes, so you try to make one up. You try to logically understand how someone in their right mind could reject you. You are adorable, aren't you? Lovable, strong, funny, kind, heart as big as Kansas? *Yes, that's you!* And still, sometimes, people will just not like you. Men will reject you. Women will hurt you. You may not win the game or have the fame—and that is just tough luck. Or, rather, reality. You don't like everyone else, do you? You have preferences, you have desires, and that is the beauty of free will.

Do I wish there was an easy answer as to why men promise to call and then don't? Obviously. But there isn't one. And this isn't about people who don't keep their promises—this is about you, trying to take action in your own life, not punishing yourself by taking negative action after an event like a bad date.

On behalf of your self-image, your self-esteem, and your self-respect: Get your body out of the kitchen and your mind out of the Language of Fat, and show yourself some more love! You don't have to punish yourself just because someone has disappointed you or rejected you. I know it might feel like it takes the sting away—to binge and then diet and then binge again—but just because it is a familiar pattern doesn't make it a good pattern. Trust me, this comes from a woman who had her own love affair with Ben and Jerry after every bad date. It is a momentary calm, followed by a lot of consequence. And I am not talking about weight gain; I am talking about continuing to self-loathe and not being able to take care of yourself.

Put Down the Sweets, Pick Up a Pen

One of the things you need to bring into any relationship you create is the ability to know yourself and take care of yourself. If you're strong and clear and loving, you can be strong and clear and loving to another person. Rather than lashing out each time you are hurt and out of control, put down the sweets and pick up a pen—write down your rage, scribble it, paint it, sing it, scream it into a pillow, breathe it away in meditation, dance it out of you, do anything except restrict and binge over it.

Someday My Prince Will Come

It is tempting to think that once you lose some weight, or get in shape, or change your looks, your knight in shining armor will appear. It is also tempting to stay focused on a fantasy version of a relationship, one that happens five pounds from now, versus living in the present and finding the most loving and lovable parts of who you are. Without this self-knowledge you remain at a disadvantage because you will continue to live your life in fast-forward, waiting to fall in love . . . when you are finally perfect.

I don't think weight gets in the way of falling in love. I think false illusion, excuses, fear, and societal messaging get in the way of *feeling* love. You may have been sold a story when you were a little girl that Prince Charming would come for you, and that for every deserving woman there is another equally deserving man (or woman). If you look closely, you'll see that the princesses in those stories are white, slender, (usually) blond, and always waiting for the man to show up and rescue them.

I refuse to buy this story anymore. Falling in love is glamorized in the movies, in magazines, and on television. In real life it looks more like this: A woman who is learning about herself, living her life fully in the world, enjoying each moment and accepting herself, ultimately ends up attracting a very appropriate person to call her partner. There is no height/weight requirement with love. Love is inside of you. If you can't accept yourself, you can't attract someone who will accept you.

We've All Done It

We've all believed that if we were just a little more toned, tanned, or taut, we could snag the person we have our eye on. One of the most dangerous consequences in speaking the Language of Fat is that it attempts to make a logical connection between your physical appearance and your worth as a person. And just as it is easier to speak about being fat than it is to really feel and express deep emotions, it is often easy to believe that something as important and uncontrollable as love is just waiting for you—if only you would lose some weight! Of course, we are more susceptible to this messaging when it comes to love, because it is every human being's primary desire to feel loved.

I have no problem with people setting healthful goals to increase vitality. But I do have a problem with a woman losing weight to attract a man. Your weight is unimportant compared with the larger issues of respect, friendship, and emotional intimacy.

Let Yourself Be Seen

It is a wild feeling to really be seen in a relationship. It feels equal parts vulnerable and exhilarating. It is so tempting to cling to your past pains and allow them to be a buffer against letting people in. When you spend so much time focusing on your body, your insecurities, and your shortcomings, you are spending less time investing in your relationships. Everyone comes into a connection carrying some baggage. I don't believe you will ever be traveling without at least a light carry-on in your life.

According to a new survey, women say they feel more comfortable undressing in front of men than they are undressing in front of other women. They say that women are too judgmental, where, of course, men are just grateful!
—Jay Leno

Dear Jess,

    I am a curvy specimen with hips, a bust, and a butt! I am a full-figured woman, and it has taken me many years to truly like my body and love my spirit. I am usually in a good mood, enjoy my job, and feel generally optimistic about life. Problem is, I am thirty-five and have been in only a handful of real relationships. My parents and even my friends always come to the same conclusion as to why. They think if I lost weight, I might attract love in my life, as they believe that the "really good men" are attracted to thinner women. They aren't really rude about it, but they do bring it up a lot! What do you think, Jess? Are my curves scaring men away?

    Yours in curvyhood, Desiree

Really good men are everywhere, and *your* really good man will appear when it is the right time. The really good men are not around the corner at the skinny store. They are out there doing their thing, waiting to cross your curvy-girl path. Your curves will not scare men away. Perhaps you've just been attracted to men who were not comfortable being with a woman who feels strong and is outspoken. Perhaps you were looking to form relationships with men who remained on the surface. It is too easy to blame it on the curves when we are feeling out of control and at a loss for answers.

We could spend forever on the issue of relationships and body image, as they are two of the most crucial topics in your life. They are the most common areas for women to give away their sense of empowerment in favor of the idea that happiness is just around the corner. It is so much easier to think of your *perfect* mate and your *perfect* body hanging out together in some *perfect* universe, waiting for you to crack the secret code that opens the door to all your (skinny) hopes and (super-skinny) dreams! But, my friends, the only person you have control over in your life is you. You can only be who you are. People will like you, or they won't.

When you are paying attention to the language you speak, the thoughts you think, and the actions you take, then you are preparing to get into the best relationship you will ever have . . . a relationship with yourself.

> *How many cares one loses when one decides not to be something but to be someone.* —Coco Chanel

---

Relationship Sabotage Checklist

- Do you feel you will finally be in a loving relationship once you lose weight?

- Do you use the Language of Fat in your current relationships?

- Do you find that your body image keeps you from being intimate and close with your partner?

- Are you with someone who does not respect your body (for example: commenting on your weight, insults, pressure to change your body)?

- Do you use your body image as a reason to not be in a relationship at all?

- Do you and your partner bond only when speaking the Language of Fat?

- Do you spend more time thinking about food and

? ? fat than you spend thinking about your partner?

■ Are you convinced that once your partner changes his or her body that your relationship will change?

■ Do you use your low self-esteem to manipulate people into paying attention to you? (Example: "Do you think that girl is prettier than me?")

■ Are you waiting to lose weight before you have sex with the lights on?

If you answered yes to any of these questions, then keep reading: We have more work to do.

TAKE ACTION

1. Remember that the way you treat your body is the way you will treat your relationships.

2. Write down in your notebook or journal the first five words that come to mind about your current relationship. Then write down the first five words that come to mind about how you feel about your body. See if there is any overlap. What you write down may surprise you!

3. You can only control yourself, so give up false expectations of others and look at the truth of your relationship.

4. Monitor the use of the Language of Fat in your relationships. Make sure it isn't impeding your intimacy and connection.

5. Don't blame it on your curves.

6. Remember that when you love yourself, you will attract more love into your life. Sounds simple, because it is.

7. For further discovery, keep a relationship inventory in your journal or notebook. Make three columns and fill in the details as illustrated in the example below.

RELATIONSHIP	HOW I FEEL	WHAT I AM WILLING TO DO
(Write name)	(Write feelings)	(Write action steps)

Refer to the relationship inventory when you get stuck, and remember that you can also use this inventory in evaluating the relationship you have with yourself.

Chapter Five

"Thunder Thighs Run in My Family!"

Most commonly heard:
In Mom's well-intentioned explanations of family genetics; rattling around in the corners of your head; and coming out of the mouth of your Aunt Edna, who is trying to justify why she is on her fifth donut.

Translation(s):
Can mean any of the following, but is not limited to:

"I hate my thighs, and as my daughter so will you!"

"I don't feel comfortable with my body or food choices, so I am going to straddle you with a made-up family legacy, to bring you closer to me in this discomfort."

"I'm not sure how to connect with you about what you're feeling, so I am just going to give you this surface excuse to tide things over for now."

"I am going to pass on to you exactly what my mother used to say to me."

Parents Know How to Push Our Buttons, Because They Installed Them

It doesn't take very much from them. A look, a nod, a breath even, and we find ourselves reeling in ballistic angst about something our parents did to us when we were younger. We have to remember that before they installed our buttons, our parents had parents who installed theirs. And when we have children, we will install their buttons as well.

Sorry, but no one comes out unscathed from having parents or from being a parent. It is our collective destiny. And you know what? Your parents did the very best job they could with what they had. They weren't much older than you are now (maybe even younger), and if you're still deciding whether or not to forgive your mother for making you wear taffeta to your sister's graduation or forgive your father for constantly embarrassing you in front of your friends, you have to, at some point in your life, let go a little about the parent damage. Everyone has it.

Many of you grew up in families that spoke the Language of Fat. Whether your family bestowed on you a childhood nickname that you still can't shake ("Tubby Wubby," "Whale's Tail," "Thunder Thighs"), or your mother always put you on a diet, or you had a stepfather who prided himself on appearing "perfect," you have to understand the link between your body image and family dynamics before you can ever expect to get over it.

It is an incredibly tricky feat to try to get someone to engage in a new kind of interaction with his or her family. By the time you reach a young age, you have patterns worked out with your parents. You ingest their beliefs, their thoughts, and their opinions about the world until you're old enough to make some of your own.

Your family can pass down the legacy of body-loathing to generation after generation if you let them. You have to drop all blame and shame, and take a solid look into your family relationships. Explore whether you think they might be sabotaging your emotional and physical health.

Ashley's Story

It was a war. Thunder thighs versus Ashley from the Midwest, a strong-willed, floppy-banged teenager who knew exactly who her enemy was. I met her in the back of a high school auditorium after a workshop. She had not an ounce of extra weight on her legs, let alone any excess skin, unsightly hair, or spider veins, the most common weapons thunder thighs use when they wage war. Ashley didn't have any of it. In fact, she had, as far as I could tell, very muscular, lean legs that showed the strength she'd had to develop and the quadriceps squats she'd had to endure to become a state soccer champion.

"Who told you that thunder thighs run in your family, Ashley?" I asked.

"My mother. She reminds me all the time that I will get her thunder thighs if I ever stop working out. She reminds me of it when I don't want to go to practice or when I want to eat an ice-cream sundae. She always holds over my head the fact that she and her sisters have big legs."

"How does this make you feel, Ashley?"

Looking down at her legs as though she were going to concede defeat in this body war, she said, "It makes me feel like a failure already. Because I'm not sure yet if I want to be a professional soccer player. But I don't want to look like my mom. And I don't want to have thunder thighs."

Ashley was voicing a perfect example of what it feels like to have the Language of Fat passed down from parent to child. She had been encouraged to be concerned about a supposed genetic predisposition to large thigh size for women in her family. Could there be truth to her mother's claims that the women in their clan grow fuller legs than they'd like? Perhaps. Was it going to be Ashley's lot in life to have the same feelings about her body? Not necessarily.

Knowing the slippery slope I was about to climb, I asked Ashley what she would say to her mother if she could say anything without getting into trouble. She thought for a minute and then said, "I would want to tell her that I am not her! I am not her and I am not going to go on the crazy diets and obsess about my legs like she does. I would tell her to leave my thighs alone!"

Hallelujah! How many of you wish you could have told your overly doting parents to back off when it came to their incessant meddling in your food choices, your exercise habits, or your clothing preferences? And I suspected that telling her mom to leave her thighs alone was something Ashley thought about a lot.

Ashley's mom may not have been aware that she was slowly poisoning her daughter's vision of her body, helping to create such paranoia that, at the age of fifteen, Ashley was viewing the rest of her life as just a period of time where her thighs would grow larger and larger.

Ashley felt incredibly doomed, and quite aware of the fact that her body was her enemy. That sent conflicting messages to her because, as an athlete, she needed to work with her body to accomplish her footwork on the field. But inside, Ashley feared that anything she ate—or even looked at—

would add weight to her body. And what did it mean exactly for her to inherit that family legacy? She said it would mean that "I would always be complaining and unhappy." Plain and simple, on some level that is how she saw her mother's relationship to her body: complaining and unhappy. And that was something Ashley was determined to escape.

Watch Your Language, Mom and Dad

I know most of what comes out of parents' mouths is well intentioned, but it is time to really take a look at what you say to children.

- How do you describe your bodies, your emotions, your feelings?
- Do you describe people by the size of their bodies?
- Do you make fun of people based on weight?
- Do you berate yourself in front of children?

The way you talk about yourself can easily become the way they talk about themselves. They're programmed by your self-esteem before they begin to form their own.

If you pinch and pull at your skin in front of your children, if you ask your spouse or your child if you "look fat," if you bad-mouth yourself in front of your mirror or show obsession or fear around food—any of these things are contagious behaviors for your children. You can't expect to tell your children that they should have high self-esteem and feel good about themselves when you don't. You have to walk your talk as parents, and show through action.

> *God could not be everywhere,*
> *so he created mothers.*
> *—Jewish proverb*

It's a Mother-Daughter Thing

A girl's relationship with her mother is a complicated and beautiful thing. We are born from her body, literally connected to her in the womb in a way that ties us early on to her nourishment: A baby feeds from its mother to live. It makes sense, then, that body-image issues and food issues between mothers and daughters are so prominent in our society. You are still feeding off your mother, in need of her approval, support, and unconditional love. Some of you get it. Some don't.

My own relationship with my mother has taken many shapes and forms over my life. Early on I began dieting with my mom, becoming her body-loathing buddy. And I hated the way my mother hated her body. So I turned her inner rage and dissatisfaction about her body toward my own body and developed eating disorders that rocked my adolescent world. What I eventually learned about my mother—who now, at sixty, is zooming along in life with a healthier mindset about her physical shape—is that her own body-loathing was formed at an early age.

At the age of nine, she remembers, she was taken to the family doctor for a checkup. The doctor revealed that she was about fifteen pounds overweight. He immediately urged my grandmother to put her on a diet to take off the weight. What the doctor blatantly failed to notice was that my mother had matured early and was in fact going through puberty. So the extra weight gain was normal and would most likely work itself out as she continued to grow up.

But it was too late. By the time the doctor passed down the declaration for weight loss, my mother was sucked into the shameful and restrictive world of dieting. This pattern of binge-ing, restricting, and punishing herself for being overweight—for being "bad," in her point of view as a child—ended up staying with her for more than fifty years.

Family Style

Dear Jess,

Help! My mother is driving me crazy! She criticizes me because of my weight. She reads the menu to me when we go to the restaurant; she tells me what she thinks would be "healthy" to order. She is constantly on a diet, but she doesn't have *any* weight to lose. And I am not alone in my misery. She makes my poor father go on a diet with her. I swear, even the dog is on a diet. (I'm not kidding!)

She makes everyone in her life crazy with her incessant complaining about her weight. And when you try to tell her that she looks beautiful or that she doesn't need to lose any weight, she goes berserk and talks about how fat she is and how we can all stand to lose a little weight. Please help!

—Frustrated in Tennessee

Our mothers are supposed to be our infallible family leaders. But they are also women, who are just as susceptible as anyone else to the messages of weight loss and to the beauty myths that our culture carries. Mothers can be quite damaging without intending to be. It is in these good intentions that your sense of self can get crushed. You cannot fix your mother. Just as she can't fix you, and just as you can't fix anyone who isn't ready to face their issues and take some action. You will have to learn how to decode the Language of Fat with your mother—or any family member, for that matter.

You can't deal with your mother in logical terms until you realize that she is speaking another language. It's painful for a family to watch their mother/wife be disrespectful to herself. Try sitting down with your mom one-on-one and telling her that it pains you greatly to see her so obsessed with dieting. Try to speak with her in a space that is not around food and not at a time when you are really angry or fed up with her. Tell her that she may not be aware of how much her own body-loathing spills out to others. Recognize that there is something deeper going on. If your mom wants to talk about it, great. Otherwise you are going to have to learn some simple self-defense moves in how to respond to her.

The next time she tries to tell you how fat she is—or you are, or your dad is, or the dog is—you can simply say, "Mom, I don't want to speak the Language of Fat with you. What else are you feeling?"

Or you can tell her, "Mom, I love you so much, but when you speak like that it drives me nuts. Can we please talk about something other than your weight?" Use your own words, but the point is to say something in the moment and also to find time to talk in quiet, where some other truths may be revealed.

Rather than putting all the focus on losing weight, why don't you focus on repairing this relationship with your mother? If you are finding that your relationship with your mother is getting in the way of you taking care of yourself, then it is your responsibility to do something about it.

Most important, remember that you have to find some peace and solitude with your body—whether Mom approves or not.

Families are about love overcoming emotional torture. —Matt Groening

Family Meeting

For those of you who have been labeled either the "thin one" or the "fat one" in your family, find a time to talk to your family about how this description makes you feel. Be as honest as you can. Tell your family that you want them to address you as a whole person, not just a size or shape. Also express that you don't want to be compared to a different-size sibling. You don't owe anyone an apology for being born the way you are. You need to embrace the body you were born with and begin treating it with more respect.

??The Family Quiz ? ? ? ? ? ? ? ? ? ? ? ? ? ? ? ?

1. Your father spots you eyeing a piece of dessert. He says:

   a. "Go ahead, honey, enjoy it!"

   b. "I thought you were going on a diet!"

   c. "Don't eat that cake, it is full of nothing but sugar and fat!"

   d. "God, you have no control!"

2. In one single conversation with your mother, how many times does she mention your weight?

   a. Never, we talk about other things.

   b. Once or twice

   c. Five times

   d. Always—is there ever a time she doesn't mention it?

3. While dining with your mother, she:

   a. Asks you about your life and shares moments of hers.

   b. Talks about this new diet she wants to try . . . tomorrow.

   c. Talks about other people's weight or appearance.

   d. Begins planning what she is going to eat at the next meal.

4. You haven't seen your father in six months. When he greets you at the airport, the first thing he says is:

   a. "I've missed you so much!"

   b. "Wow, you look like you've put on some weight."

   c. "I guess that diet didn't work, huh?"

   d. "Have you ever met a cookie you've said no to?"

5. Name the thing you have most in common with your mother:

   a. Our wit, sense of humor, and love for shopping

   b. Our mutual disdain for our flabby arms

   c. Our shared diet tips

   d. Our desire to be thinner

6. In order to motivate you to take better care of yourself, your father:

   a. Lovingly tells you that he'd like to see you stick around awhile.

   b. Offers to buy you a new wardrobe if you lose ten pounds.

   c. Practices tough love and won't talk to you till you get in shape.

   d. Makes jokes at your expense.

If you answered anything other than "a" to any question in this quiz, you may have the beginnings of what is affectionately known as "Mama Drama" or a "Daddy Dilemma," the prevalent and unfortunate bonding of mothers, fathers, and daughters through the Language of Fat. These dramas and dilemmas have been known to ruin otherwise healthy relationships, hurt people's feelings, and basically drive you crazy! Approach them with the intention of decoding the language that is keeping your relationship mired in this misguided bonding. As with any of the advice you are given, it is up to you to choose to take action.

? ?

I grew up to have my father's looks, my father's speech patterns, my father's posture, my father's walk, my father's opinions, and my mother's contempt for my father. —Jules Feiffer

No Family Is Perfect

Families make and break you. Within your family I'm sure you can find unending peace, comfort, and safety. You can also find dashes of insanity, neuroticism, and codependence. If you are lucky, you will have a family that blends both of those worlds. You know that your mom and dad, your sister and brother, are not perfect. You are far from perfect too. There has to come a point in your life when you begin to take responsibility for who you are as an adult. You can choose to wear your childhood hurts like an iron-on patch, covering up the wounded thighs and berated belly, or you can choose to use them as growing experiences and take the risk to decide for yourself what your belief systems are.

BELIEF INVENTORY

BELIEFS	FROM WHERE?	WHAT DO I THINK?

Grab your journal and make a chart with three columns, with the headings above.

1. Under "Beliefs" write down a belief that you have. For instance, "Thunder thighs run in my family."

2. In the next column write down where you got that belief—your mom, your dad, society, friends, etc.

3. In the final column write down how that belief makes you feel. Just let your thoughts flow (perhaps for the first time), and see what you come up with.

Casting Call

Family is like a big theatrical production. Everyone plays a role. What is yours? Are you:

- The sensitive one?
- The baby?
- The spoiled brat?
- The angry one?
- The depressed one?
- The jock?
- The superstar?
- The smart one?
- The fat one?
- The thin one?
- The one always struggling with your weight?

When these roles get set in stone in your psyche or self-esteem, they can be hard to shake. That doesn't mean you have to punish yourself because you have a different set of genes from, say, your sister or your brother. What do you want to do? Go crawl back into the womb and demand a do-over? Okay, so you look like your father. Okay, so you are not as thin as your mother and sister. But who are *you*? Spend time focusing on who you are instead of who you are not.

The family—that dear octopus from whose tentacles we never quite escape, nor, in our inmost hearts, ever quite wish to.
—Dodie Smith

"Thunder Thighs Run in My Family!"

Walk Your Talk

I met Tracy three months before she was due to give birth to her first child. She was having a hard time fighting off the negative body talk she was experiencing the further along she was in her pregnancy. She said people, even complete strangers, were always coming up to her and touching her and telling her that she was "so big." Eventually it began to wear her out. Tracy had been a survivor of physical abuse at a young age and grew up with an abusive mom who rarely said a kind word about her weight. Instead, her mother would tell everyone that she had a nickname for her kid, "fatso." It was humiliating, and Tracy became very skilled in speaking the Language of Fat as a way of continuing the punishment and pain.

Tracy found out she was going to give birth to a girl. She was in a loving marriage and had not spoken to her mother in years. But as she grew closer to bringing her baby into the world, she began to hear her mother's negative talk in her mind. She had fears about how she could raise a girl in the world who would feel empowered and strong, and not fall prey to speaking the Language of Fat.

She noticed that body image issues were rampant when you are pregnant. Everyone has an opinion of how much weight an expectant mother should gain, and everyone who has been pregnant obsessively talks about how much their bodies changed when they were pregnant and how "fat" most of them had gotten. Tracy even noticed this with her closest friends. They would tell her horror stories about their stretch marks and the lingering weight they weren't able to lose. She realized that even pregnant women can speak the

96

Language of Fat incessantly. And that made sense to her, because pregnancy is such a unique experience; not everyone can share in it, but they can all think they understand the feeling of being fat. And for some women it became an easy way to mask the other intense feelings about bringing a baby into the world.

Tracy decided that she was going to stop the cycle of body-loathing before it was passed on to another generation in her family. She and her husband signed an oath together that they would not utter words in the Language of Fat in their house. They wanted to make sure their home was filled with only positive body talk.

This was completely different from the way Tracy had been brought up. Today she understands that she won't be the perfect mother and that she will make mistakes. But if she can just do it a little better than her mother did, she thinks she will be making a big impact. And she will.

Tracy's experience reminds me that nothing that happened to you in your childhood is set in stone. Your legacies and impact on the world are being created in each and every moment.

Having a family is like having a bowling alley installed in your brain.
—Martin Mull

TAKE ACTION

1. Remember that parents know how to push your buttons because they installed them.

2. Watch what you say in front of children, and watch how you treat your body in front of children. They pick up on your words and mimic your actions!

3. Choose to no longer speak the Language of Fat with your family. Find something else to talk about.

4. Take a risk! Have an honest talk with your family members about how their language or behavior impacts you.

5. Discover your own belief systems by using the Belief Inventory.

6. Remember that the role you are cast in within your family unit can change. You have the power to create your own legacy by making new choices!

Chapter Six

"I'd Be So Happy If I Looked Like a Celebrity!"

Most commonly heard:

In conversations with yourself, your best friends, your boyfriend, your husband, your family, or your roommate. Also in the private thoughts that jump around your brain as you watch television, read magazines, or see a movie.

Translation(s):

Can mean any of the following, but is not limited to:

"Fantasizing about a celebrity's life allows me to escape my everyday problems."

"I believe I am not good enough as is, so I choose to compare myself to an unrealistic ideal, believing it will bring me happiness."

"I am putting off living my life today because I am so wrapped up in the images being sold to me by the media."

The Cult of Celebrity

Everyone does it—covets celebrity, dreaming about trading lives with the rich and famous. Everyone visualizes how handsome their lovers would be (you have "lovers" when you are famous), how beautiful their wardrobe would be, and how perfect their body would be. For a brief but brilliant moment this allows you to escape from the day-to-day schlep and trudge called your life. This role-playing gives you permission to fantasize about a life with seemingly no worries other than what fabulous party to go to, what fabulous person to date, and what fabulous city to go to on vacation (you are always on vacation when you are famous).

And it makes sense. It really does. Fantasy is good. It is healthy. It is normal and natural to daydream and allow your mind to expand with pleasurable possibilities.

And yet some of us go overboard, poring over countless numbers of tabloid magazines, hoping to catch a glimpse of our favorite pop star's cellulite-dimpled rear end or the latest "it" girl's unshaven armpits. We compare our hair, lips, eyes, clothing, and skin color to those we see plastered on billboards and at bus stops. But when does celebrity curiosity give way to a deeper issue? How much does this cult of celebrity truly impact our body image and self-esteem?

There is nothing wrong with being interested in the life of your favorite actor, actress, or musician. But it can go wrong if your interest and intrigue turns into an obsession that fuels the Language of Fat and further sends you down a spiraling path of body-loathing and jealousy, which interrupts your real life.

And the blame does not rest squarely on the malnourished shoulders of today's celebrities. They are pawns in a larger corporate game of selling self-worth in pills, shakes, clothing, makeup, and other products, all designed to make you feel "happy." The messaging is not so subtle anymore. Major movie stars hawk anything that lines their bank accounts, and the word "branding" gets bandied about by twelve-year-olds. You are savvy enough to know that when you see your favorite celebs on the morning-show circuit, they are there to promote their latest album, not to debate social injustices. And that is *okay*. Really, it is. The key to living in this slick, celebrity-gossip-fueled society is to be smart about what you are watching and what you are taking into your psyche. The more conscious you can become about the images being presented to you, the better equipped you will be to make your own decisions and form your own opinions.

Break It Down

There is a lot of tricky and dangerous language imbedded in our media, and it partners up with messaging that aims to keep you distant from yourself, so that you will feel bad and want more and buy more, in pursuit of that elusive happiness.

- **Step one:** Recognize that you are being sold to all the time. All the time. It may be a CD, a TV show, a food product, or just the general brand and image of a celebrity or sports superstar. The main goal is to get you to buy something by convincing you that it will make you happy.
- **Step two:** Realize that your happiness does not lie outside of yourself. The only surefire way to feel more happy and content in your life is to create happy and contented moments. And you do that not by hating yourself into submission so you are purchasing everything thrown your way, but by believing that you possess the power to change

your life. Not the chick on that new reality show. Or the famous Grammy-winning songstress. You.

- **Step three:** Take an honest look at your views and belief systems about the media, advertising, and celebrity obsession. Discover just how much of an impact these outer influences have on your self-esteem.

? ?The Celebrity Reality Check ? ? ? ? ? ? ? ? ? ?

So how do you know if you have crossed the line into a lapsed reality that has you so concerned with the latest scandal involving the underage TV star and her "manager" that you have forgotten to feed the cat and kids? How do you know if you have just a healthy, mild obsession with the hottest fashionista's restaurant choices? Take this quiz.

True or False:

1. You cannot name the current secretary of defense but can name all of the characters on *The O.C.*, including quirky bio notes like which actor loves chocolate ice cream in the morning.

2. When you look at a picture of your favorite female celebrity, your first thought is, "Wow, she looks amazing." And your second thought is, "I am so *fat*."

3. You find yourself talking about the latest "it" girl's romantic conquests more than two times a day.

4. You compulsively buy the latest fashion magazines and make lists of the clothes you'll buy when you can fit into them.

5. You are only aware of current events when a beautiful movie star goes on national TV to talk about them.

6. You have been known to collect pictures of today's hottest celeb couple, and then insert your picture next to your "future husband."

7. You go on whatever diet your favorite actress talks about in her morning TV interview.

8. You spend more than five minutes a day wishing you were someone famous.

9. You won't wear something until you have seen it captured on the pages of a popular magazine being worn by a popular celebrity.

10. You really believe your life would be perfect if you had your favorite celeb's body.

If you answered "True" to even one of these questions, then it is time for a media reality intervention.

We Are the Media

I am *so* not antimedia. I love the media. I work in the media. The media has huge and terrific powers, if used for good and not evil. And the media is not some superhuman group of people or even a faceless, nameless corporation. You are a part of the media. There are those of you who make it, those who write for it, pose for it, sell through it, purchase it, and worship it. You serve as part of the same food chain and ecosystem. The goal to aim for is a balanced harmony of both media and self-esteem. And this is not the inherent cycle of things as they stand right now. Our current media is not aimed at bolstering your self-esteem, nor, some would argue, will it ever be the goal of the media to make you feel good about yourself. That said, we have to enter this relationship with the media and the cult of celebrity with a little more scrutiny and self-protection. Always remember, though, that self-responsibility is the ultimate tool you have for changing the way you view and interact with the world.

Celebrity is never more admired than by the negligent. —William Shakespeare

---

Your relationship with the media is almost as complicated as your relationship to your body. The media is a major contributing factor to our personal issues of low self-esteem—like a background of really loud noise that makes it difficult to hear the softer inner voice of truth. And though we can be impacted by it, manipulated by it, and have strong emotions about it, the media does not cause eating disorders. Instead, it reflects that back to us.

The media reflects how you feel about your body (ashamed, always dissatisfied), and it reflects your place in the world (you don't have anything really meaningful to say, so shut up and diet!) by showing you your darker side. And it is a personal statement. Not an institutionalized statement. Why? Because people create these images. *People.* Human beings who are living in a world that we have all created.

She Doesn't Even Look Like Her!

Until about ten years ago I always thought "the media" was some giant dark force out there that just miraculously delivered the images I saw. The notion that we are all responsible for the media was born when I was a guest at a celebrity photo shoot for a brand-new women's magazine. It was here that my veils of ignorance were lifted.

The woman gracing the cover was famous for her body and the tune she could carry. In that order. I had seen her body on the cover of so many magazines and blown up on billboards that when I saw her in person I hardly recognized her. She was much shorter than I had imagined. The first veil was lifted: When you view someone fifty feet above ground on a billboard or blown up on a movie screen, they appear so much larger than in real life.

Duh, makes sense.

I watched her as she went to hair and makeup. She had four people working on her at one time: Two for hair, two for makeup. Then I watched as the photographer directed his crew to hang lights. Ten people were on hand to set the lighting up so that you would think the glow across her cheeks was just a natural sparkle. I walked over to wardrobe and eyed the pair of shorts she was going to wear. A pair of leather shorts had been made for her, cut and sewn specifically to her measurements. Veil number two: The clothing that we see on models and actors in magazines is almost always designed for them or tailored to fit their bodies perfectly.

Our cover model came out of hair and makeup and already looked like a goddess, and a very different version of the woman who had walked in the door a few hours earlier. Veil number three: The right hair and makeup can be much better than plastic surgery!

She changed into those shrunken leather shorts, which was when we encountered our first tragedy of the day. The shorts didn't fit. Apparently our model had eaten something in

Hollywood's Big Fat Lies

- Anyone who doesn't look like they need an IV is "curvy."
- It's okay to tell the public about your plastic surgery and implants, but don't you dare tell them about your depression, bipolar behavior, or eating disorders. Mental illness is, like, so out!
- Dark circles, gaunt cheeks, hair loss, and a new set of veneers are all a part of "getting healthy."
- Don't get old. There is no greater damage done to your career than the damage done by turning thirty. Just don't do it.
- Always shrink, never expand. Shrinking your body gives your career a boost. Expanding gets you a diet product endorsement deal.

between the time of her fitting and her shoot. Some genius assistant had an idea to cut open a slit in the back of her shorts so her rear end could hang out a bit and the shorts could be moved over her hips. Veil number four: Humiliating things happen even to gorgeous celebrities.

Once the shorts were snugly in place over her hips, the photographer gave her his first set of directions: "Suck in your stomach, tight, tight, tighter." Veil number five: It doesn't matter that you are an already slim celebrity—you will still be ordered to suck in your stomach.

The photographer still wasn't happy, so he ordered another two assistants to go and tape her back with duct tape. Yes, you read that correctly. Two men used duct tape to tape the "back fat" (I call it skin) that she supposedly had, so that it would create a deeper indent around her waist when he shot her head-on. "I want you to look superb," he announced. Veil number six: Sometimes celebrities don't have the power to call all the shots.

So that makes four people who did her makeup and hair, one who cut the slit in her shorts, two who taped her "back fat" together, ten who hung the lights, one photographer, and three assistants—a grand total of twenty-one people who put this look together. And you fork out for the magazine and wonder why you don't look like her? *She* doesn't even look like her! Veil number seven: What you purchase on the cover of magazines are manufactured images. Not real.

Once those veils were gone, it allowed me to feel more empowered with my decisions about what I purchase, and most important, about how I let the things I purchase affect me. I was a willing partner in that transaction. So are you. You can choose to give your power away to everything you see, or you can choose to really see the truth behind the imagery.

The whole celebrity culture thing—I am fascinated by, and repelled by, and yet I end up knowing about it. —Anderson Cooper

---

Celebrities Are People Too

You believe celebrities have perfect lives because you are told they have perfect lives. You are shown their perfect lives. And they work very hard, sometimes, to pretend they are superhuman. You are trained to believe that they don't have the issues you face as a noncelebrity, because it sells more products if you believe that they are better than you. That they have some special insight about life that you don't. Because when you feel that they have the power, you will go see their movie, buy the shampoo they are selling, or continue to buy the magazines they're profiled in. But remember that they are just people, and that means they have the same emotional, physical, and spiritual difficulties that you or I may have.

What's Really Wrong?

It's normal to want to escape—for a bit—into the glamorous life of a superstar. But it is not normal if escaping creates feelings that you are less worthy and uninteresting compared to your favorite celebrity. To pretend as though you are nothing in comparison to him or her is to sell yourself short. If you are dissatisfied with your life, then do something to spice it up. Are you in a career you hate? A relationship that is not giving to you? Or are you just spending an inordinate amount of time on a fantasy to avoid confronting emotional issues in your own life?

Perhaps you believe that money, looks, and fame equal perfection. That may be your belief system right now. But what about **honesty, integrity, friendship,** and **love**? How high on your list do those qualities rank? Do you have people that you love? **Admire**? Have deep friendships with? Are you a woman of your word? Do you treat people **kindly** and **fairly**? You may want to really think about what you have going for you now, in *your* perfect life, because that is all you've got. Don't get blinded by **wealth** or **fame** or **beauty**. They are all fleeting qualities.

Don't Blame the Posters

Dear Jess,

My boyfriend, Charles, has posters and calendars of a supermodel all over his dorm room. He doesn't think there is anything wrong or sexist about it, since he says he just likes to look at "nice things." But whenever I go to visit him in his room, I begin to feel really unattractive and fat. I keep thinking that if this is his ideal woman, as she is plastered all over his walls, then he must not think I am attractive. I mean, he has more pictures of this model than he does of me! How can I discuss this with him without him thinking I am being too sensitive?

—Randy

Some men put these images up around them because that is what they feel is encouraged by their peers. They may not give much thought to the impact that these oversexualized and unrealistic images have on women. Don't be afraid to communicate that to the man in your life. Don't make excuses for his lack of awareness and don't play the victim, just sit down and tell him how you feel. Explain to him that women aren't products or pictures; they're people. Try to give him some examples of what it would feel like for him if you had the same thing in your room. You can't outlaw what men look at, but if they are interested in you as a complete person, they can afford the time to listen to your feelings.

Celebrity worship and hero worship should not be confused. Yet we confuse them every day, and by doing so we come dangerously close to depriving ourselves of all real models. —Daniel J. Boorstin

?? What You See Is Not What You Get ??????

When you feel triggered by something you see, start by asking yourself these questions:

- Have you found yourself having feelings of being "unattractive and fat" before? If so, when do these feelings seem to arise?
- Have you noticed other triggers in your life that cause the same reaction? Perhaps there is something else you want to communicate in your relationship and you don't feel listened to or respected.
- Are there times when your partner's language about other women is sexist and demeaning? What do you typically do about it?
- Are you getting what you need emotionally in your relationship?
- Do you feel honored, loved, and adored?

By asking yourself these questions you take the blame away from the visual image and move more toward self-discovery and responsibility.

Don't Judge a Book by Its Cover

Nothing that you purchase is in its natural state. Not the cover of a magazine, a CD or DVD case, even the picture on the back of this book. All of it has been doctored or airbrushed to some degree. Why? Because you are plopping down your hard-earned money, and the people who create these products want you to think it was money well spent. The products need to appear perfect, or at least better than anything you could come up with in your garage, so that you place some value on them and hopefully buy more. As we have discussed, this is the basic principle with all media: to sell you things. So the one way you can exert control as a target demographic is to speak out with the way you spend your money. Oftentimes, greenbacks yell louder than actual voices do.

Walk Your Talk

Dear Jess,

You might laugh, but I consider myself a recovering beauty-product junkie. I mean it. If it came in a tube and was gonna whiten, lift, plump, or color anything on my face, I would buy it in bulk. I was spending a lot of money on things that promised to make me prettier, and I noticed that I was feeling just the opposite. The more I bought, the uglier I felt. It was like I was always one step away from finding the perfect product that would turn my life around.

One day I was feeling so bad about myself that when I came home, I broke into tears. When I went into the bathroom to get a tissue, I noticed what the tops of my counters looked like. They were a mess! Nothing but bottles, brushes, and makeup. Some of it I hadn't even opened yet. And then it hit me. I was really unhappy buying all of these products, and I had to do something about it. So I began to pare down everything that wasn't necessary to my everyday grooming. I started a savings account, and when I am tempted to buy a product, I put the money in the account instead.

Then I came up with a way to surround myself with inspiration throughout the day. I took an old compact mirror and taped a tiny slip of paper to the mirror. The paper says, "You are beautiful," and every time I go to apply my lipstick or check myself out, I see that message. It is such a small gesture, but it has made a big impact on my life. Now the products I buy also double as a brief reminder of my worth. I wanted to share this tip with you in hopes that you would share it with others.

—Vanessa

If you choose to, you can decode the media around you so that you are preserving your well-being and self-esteem. You can also put your money behind products and companies that stand for what you believe in.

There are so many little things you can do in your day to navigate through the enticing and addictive world of advertising and media. It doesn't mean you have to reject it all and go live in a cave somewhere. But it does mean that you can find strong, creative ways to rethink the impact the media has on your life.

There are many ways to make your voice heard.

Americans spend more money each year on beauty than they do on education.
—The Economist, May 24, 2003

TAKE ACTION

1. Ask yourself: Is my celebrity obsession taking over my life in any way? Am I giving away my personal power and belief system to a fantasy image?

2. Become more media savvy. Know that the target goal is to sell you something and that what you see has been air-brushed or doctored to some degree.

3. Take personal responsibility; remember that the media is made up of human beings. Find where you are a contributor and consumer to the messages you receive. Then decide what you are willing to do about it.

4. Don't hide behind the cult of celebrity as an excuse to dodge your relationship issues. Pay attention to your real life.

5. Remember that the Language of Fat is imbedded in a lot of messages you receive through the media. Continue to decode the images and the language.

6. Turn your existing products into powerful tools of inspiration and validation. Put a slip of paper with your favorite empowering saying, such as "I'm beautiful!" or "I am worth it!" over the mirrored portion of your compact. So whenever you open your compact, you will see that positive message.

7. Purchase things that make you feel good. If what you are buying makes you feel like crap, don't buy it! Your dollar can speak louder than your voice.

I'm beautiful!   **I am worth it!**

"Once I Lose Some Weight, My Career Will Take Off!"

Most commonly heard:
In excuses and reasons why we aren't where we want to be in life.

Translation(s):
Can mean any of the following, but is not limited to:

"I will put off taking care of my needs, desires, and dreams today as I focus on some future fantasy of what my life will be like when I am thin!"

"I have no idea what I want to be in the world, so instead I will focus on my weight, because that is controllable."

"I am scared of my potential, so I will sabotage it by constantly thinking about my appearance."

Be the Change You Wish to See in the World

It is incredibly tempting to blame your weight for everything. It is incredibly tempting to become an expert in body-loathing instead of really taking a risk in the world. Gandhi once said,

"Be the change you wish to see in the world." But before you can be a change in the world, you have to see yourself in the world. Too often, women don't see themselves in the world because they are too busy focusing on their weight and appearance. It is more of a challenge to focus on who you are *being* than what you are *doing*. For some people body image has not only held them back from creating the life they desire, but it has robbed them of feeling true passion about their life.

??????????????????????????????????????

- Has dieting become your full-time job?
- Is body-loathing and low self-esteem your full-time hobby?
- Is learning about the newest weight loss plans, supplements, and exercise equipment your version of doing "homework"?
- Has your fascination and focus on losing weight gotten in the way of your job?

??????????????????????????????????????

Some women I know aggressively pursue the latest diet scheme rather than send out their résumés, ask the boss for a raise, or, quite frankly, do any of the necessary outreach to create the career they desire. Are you waiting to get the perfect body before you go for your dreams? Or do you feel that once you've lost weight, you will finally have the confidence you need to go back to school or quit your job? The Language of Fat can play a big part in how you view your work life and may actually be sabotaging your career plans.

There is never such an intense time of decision making about the future than on the day of college graduation. May the heavens open up and swallow you whole if you happen to be one of the students who do not have a "plan" after college. What they never tell you at graduation ceremonies is that plans change. And dreams fade and are reborn again. And that's a good thing.

Dreams Don't Have an Expiration Date

Dear Jess,

I am set to graduate from college in a few weeks, and I have no idea what I want to do with my life, really. Now the real world is smacking me in the face, and I feel like I have to figure out what I want to do and do it! I get so overwhelmed with it all that I go on these crazy diets to try to control my body, because I can't control anything else in my life. Help!

—Michelle

"What do you want to be when you grow up?" How old were you the first time you heard that question? We ask children that question all the time. It helps us put people in a category. "Oh, that's Johnny, he wants to be a gymnast." Or "This is Suzy, she is a painter." And if you are the kid who answered that question with "I don't know," you may have received this warning: "Well, you better hurry up and decide what you want to be!" As if your dreams had an expiration date.

Sometimes a hobby, sport, or activity you were good at when you were younger becomes your label, your societal name tag for who you are and what you want to be. And it's natural to be disappointed when your childhood dreams don't become adulthood realities. But there's no reason to be.

The flaw in the question "What do you want to be when you grow up?" is that the focus is usually on a job title or label. The adult version of the question is "What do you do?" with the focus clearly on the doing, not the being. People at dinner parties aren't really interested in your emotional well-being. They want to know what category to put you in, they want to know what to call you ("banker," "teacher," or "therapist"), and they want to know if there is anything they can get from you (some call this networking).

There is just as much focus on the job titles you hold as there is on the size of the body you possess. A person's worth is incredibly wrapped up in what they do as a career. What if you aren't sure what you're passionate about? When you feel like this, you are often very tempted to focus on the one thing that does seem controllable: your body.

But you have to design your life around who you are. What do you love to do in the world? What passions have you discovered? Make sure you are taking time to set small, tangible goals that you can accomplish every day. Maybe it's reading a book in your area of interest, attending a seminar, getting a mentor, volunteering in a field that interests you. Who you are in the "real" world will be created by you on a daily basis.

There are many ways to go about figuring out what you want to do, and you don't have to get it done in the next five minutes. The first job you get out of college doesn't have to last forever. You really don't need to be in a rush to figure it all out. Your dreams are supposed to change and grow with you.

---

*The closest to perfection a person ever comes is
when he fills out a job application form.*
— *Stanley J. Randall*

The Watercooler Can Be Draining

The Language of Fat doesn't just interrupt and hijack your career goals; it can also poison your work communities. It can make your everyday job environment toxic, draining, and dangerous. What do you do if you discover that the Language of Fat is being spoken by your coworkers or your boss? Well, for starters, remember that the workforce is made up of human beings. Your coworkers may be pretty steeped in speaking the Language of Fat, so the same sort of decoding that you do in your personal life can also be done at the office.

Dear Jess,

I just started a job I love. The only problem is, my office is predominantly women, and I find that they are all focused on dieting. Someone even posted dieting and nutrition tips in the bathroom! The other day I had a coworker comment to me that I would be a real "knockout" if I focused as much on my appearance and clothing style as I did on my work in the office. She said she was just kidding, but I found this comment to be really out of line, and I took it pretty personally. Any thoughts on what to do?

—Wendy

Is Your Workplace Fat-Free?

The first step is to take a good look at yourself and see if you are unwittingly speaking the Language of Fat. Do you talk about food, fat, and weight with coworkers? Do you find yourself gossiping about someone's recent weight gains or losses? It might feel like harmless gossip and watercooler conversation, but it continues to foster the Language of Fat—not only in your life but in the lives around you as well.

When you are not particularly happy in your work life, it can be a welcome distraction to concentrate on what you are eating and not eating. If you don't enjoy your job, you may find yourself sneaking snacks, binge eating, or wasting time planning dinner throughout the day. It may seem like a more exciting, rebellious, and self-medicating response to your unhappiness.

It's a vicious cycle. The more dissatisfied you are with work, and the more you don't take action to find satisfaction, the more destructive your behavior can be. This will lead you to feel upset with yourself, which in turn doesn't help you do your best work at your job, which adds to your frustration.

In the end all you'll feel is the residual impact of hurting yourself through these actions. It doesn't feel good to hide from your feelings, and you can't eat this problem away. Sometimes these experiences show up in your life to show you that you need to go in a different direction. If this is the case, and you think you may need a career switch, see a career coach or counselor. Don't allow body obsession to sabotage your work life.

How to Handle the Language of Fat at Work

1. When you are at lunch with coworkers and one of them begins to go on about her newest diet plan or another is incessantly talking about the fat grams in her sandwich, you can:

   a. Turn the topic of conversation to a current social event or news item. (But be assured, this won't stop the body talk.)

   b. Simply say, "Can we talk about something else? This kind of talk makes me uncomfortable."

   c. Laugh and say, "Do you guys realize that we always talk about food and diets together? Come on, we are a smart group of women, what else can we talk about today?"

   d. Stand up and yell, "Enough! I am so sick of wasting precious time during the day talking about how many calories are in soup. Let's move on!"

2. When your coworker is gossiping about people's weight or their appearance and tries to engage you in this banter, you can:

   a. Just ignore her and pretend you don't hear her ripping someone to shreds. (But watch your back; you could be next on her list.)

   b. Simply say, "I am not comfortable talking about people behind their backs."

   c. Laugh and say, "You know, I'm not interested in making fun of anyone today, I have so much work to do."

   d. Stand up and yell, "Enough! I am not interested in Gerta from accounting's bad haircut or Helen's obvious panty lines!"

3. If your coworkers approach you and want to talk about how fat they feel, you can:

a. Just let them degrade themselves with the Language of Fat and say nothing. (Nah, you know better than that by now. . . .)

b. Simply say, "What else is going on for you today?"

c. Laugh and say, "You know, I am tempted to speak the Language of Fat too, but I don't because there is so much more to talk about than the size and shape of our thighs, don't you think?"

d. Stand up and yell, "Enough! Why do you poison the air with such insane talk? You are a smart and successful woman—start acting like one!"

These suggestions run the range from benign neglect to full-on confrontation. You have to choose your moments carefully. So many of you are afraid to say anything for fear you will be laughed at or punished by the group. But you'll have to decide how much toxicity is being created by the constant focus and attention on the external.

Well-behaved women rarely make history.
—Laurel Thatcher Ulrich

You Have a Choice

Decoding the Language of Fat at work is just as important as decoding it in your personal life, because the same thoughts, language, and actions that limit you into believing that your life will be begin five pounds from now also prevent you from taking risks, speaking up, and pursuing dreams in your work life. In a world where so many amazing, articulate, and driven women are so wrapped up in the treacherous game of body-loathing, it's not surprising that we don't have more female CEOs or political leaders. Are you choking on all the possibilities out there for you? As women we have more choices in the workplace than ever before, so why is it that we are stuck in a rut in our lives, feeling unsure, and not passionate about anything except our physical appearance? I know many women who are prouder of their current weight than their university results.

Your career success lies not in how much you weigh, but in how much you give. How much you create. How much you offer. How much you believe in yourself and your passion.

Play the Part, Don't Worry About the Costume

I met Sasha at a friend's wedding. We instantly bonded as two of the few single girls there and started talking about her new job at a prestigious advertising agency in Chicago.

"On one hand," she said, "I am so excited because I have always dreamed of having a job at this agency. But on the other hand, I don't feel like I fit the part yet, you know what I mean?"

I didn't. So I asked her to continue.

"Well, I'm not as socially outgoing as the other women I work with, and I definitely don't have the most stylish clothes. As crazy as it sounds, everyone in my office is so well dressed,

I just feel so out-of-date and awkward. Not to mention that I've put on twenty pounds over the last year."

Here we go again. We took the fast track from passion and an emotional feeling to weight. This time we did the trip in less than sixty seconds.

She continued, "You know, I just feel like once I have a better wardrobe and a body that looks good, I will feel more confident and comfortable in front of clients."

Clearly, Sasha was speaking the Language of Fat.

She was more attached to the outfits associated with her career than to the actual job itself. She was bypassing all of the expected fear and anxiety about starting a new job—especially her dream job—and had moved into loathing her body, her clothes, and her appearance.

What I soon discovered about Sasha was that she didn't just happen to land at this powerful ad agency; she'd been actively pursued by its CEO. She was considered a superstar in the making, and a lot of people were taking notice of her talents. That scared her to death. The more people fixed their attention on Sasha, the more she shifted her attention onto her body. She fixated on her flaws instead of her triumphs. This agency hired Sasha for who she was, not for what she wore or how much she weighed.

We spent the rest of the night exploring other ways that Sasha could own her achievements and focus more on being the best version of herself that she could be. Instead of zeroing in on all the things she wanted to change about her body or her appearance, we started to speak about her passion for her career. Eventually she got it. She understood that she could choose to spend the hours of the day obsessing over not looking the part, or she could spend those hours really focusing on her job.

You can get sidetracked by speaking the Language of Fat. You can forget your goals, your dreams, and your victories. Be brave: Step out into the world and be who you are. It can be exciting to actually achieve what you want. So what is getting in the way of celebrating your accomplishments?

If you are not living life on the edge,
you are taking up too much space.
—Unknown

Your passion lies underneath all that you do. There really isn't a limit on what you can achieve in your life; the only limits are the ones you give yourself. Don't be afraid to fail. In failure you learn what works and doesn't work in your life. And remember: Achieving your goals may take days, weeks, months, or years. Allow your dreams to shift and change. Remain true to your heart. Your passion will follow.

The reason most people never reach their
goals is that they don't define them,
or ever seriously consider them
as believable or achievable.
—Denis Watley

TAKE ACTION

1. Remember, your career is happening now, not five pounds from now.

2. Do not allow another's opinion of you to rock your dreams and goals! Your success is not about what you weigh or what you look like.

3. Be careful about speaking the Language of Fat in the workplace. Practice your response to the language, just as you would in your personal life.

4. Some childhood dreams do not turn into adulthood realities, but that doesn't mean you should stop dreaming. You can have more than one dream and more than one career in a lifetime.

5. You are more than the title of your job or your education. Take a moment to focus less on the doing and more on the being.

Chapter Eight

"All of My Friends Are Hot and I'm Not!"

Most commonly heard:
In the tattered self-esteem of someone speaking the Language of Fat. Also heard in the complaints about why your friends are better at picking up guys.

Translation(s):
Can mean any of the following, but is not limited to:

"I want to fit in, I want you to like me, so I feel like the best way to get you to do that is to break myself down."

"I am not in friendships that treat me with respect, and therefore I feel terrible about myself and blame my looks."

"I am insecure in my friendships because everyone is speaking the Language of Fat, and I just want to feel accepted, so I speak it too!"

Mean Girls

"Let's have a contest and see whose legs are bigger. Come on! Line up in order of smallest to largest," Kristin decreed. It was her birthday, and everyone knew you couldn't say no to the birthday girl. We were thirteen, and I was praying not to be the last thigh standing.

Kristin's legs, of course, were the smallest of the group. I watched as girl after girl lined themselves up, eager to measure their legs against the others. No one seemed bothered by this, but then, no one had legs shaped like mine. My legs were toned and muscular when toned and muscular were so not trendy. Tiny and doll-like was in vogue in our group of friends. And on that front I lost out completely. Not only was I far from doll-like, I had a body that was shaped more like a woman's, and I had no idea that this could be a beautiful thing. Right then I just didn't want to be at the losing end of the leg competition.

It was Kristin, then Casey, then Danielle, and Jamie, and then . . . me.

"Look," said Kristin. "Extra small, small, medium, large, and extra large!" She laughed.

I wanted to kill her.

I went to sleep that night feeling betrayed by my extra-large thighs and by my friends, who seemed not to care at all that they had crushed me with this arbitrary label. They seemed content to go on and bond over their extra-small frames, while I just kept thinking about ways I could shave some fat from my thighs. When I look back at pictures of me from those years, already aware of my curves, already beginning to starve them out, I marvel at how that smart little girl could ever have looked at her legs and thought them to be anything other than long, curvy, and strong. But when you are entered into the leg-size contest at Kristin's thirteenth birthday slumber party with the hottest girls in your eighth-grade class, you just thank your lucky stars you were invited, even if your party favor is body distortion and obsessive thoughts.

The title of girl with the extra-large thighs loomed large in my life, and for the next four years I wore T-shirts to go swimming and looked at my friendships with equal parts resentment and skepticism. Would I ever feel truly safe with a group of girlfriends again? Where were my girlfriends? Where were the people who were supposed to share my deepest thoughts and secrets? Oh, I know where they were. Thanking God they didn't end up as the loser of the leg contest.

It's a Long and Winding Road

To feel protected by and connected to your girlfriends is of utmost importance. To feel like you are surrounded by women who honor and respect you—and your body—is paramount to a healthy friendship. You need to feel a sense of safety, that even through your confessions, vulnerable meltdowns, and moments of weakness, your friends will be there to support you and pick you up.

I am happy to report that now, fifteen years after Kristin's party, I have the most loving and genuine female friendships a woman could ask for. But my road to finding them has been an arduous journey of navigating through the Language of Fat and pledging at all costs to stay true to myself—even if it means disappointing someone else.

It hasn't been easy. In the past if there was an insecure, emotionally dangerous, mentally unstable girl within a ten-mile radius, I became friends with her. I went through years of inviting unhealthy friendships into my life. I credit a large part of that to the fact that I was still trying to figure out how to truly be myself around women.

In my eating disorder years I brought into my life fellow strugglers who all spoke the Language of Fat nonstop. They were more concerned with counting calories than building a mutual friendship. When I was young, I hung out with the type of friend who would steal your boyfriend in a heartbeat just to be closer to you somehow. For some reason we thought that meant that we had an intense connection as friends.

In college I soon advanced to the kinds of friends who seemed to be deeper, but when I spent time alone with them, all they could talk about was their bodies and who they wanted to share their bodies with. They found their worth in hooking up, and my dorm became like some kind of sexual Olympics.

After college I gravitated toward friends who, when I achieved great things, would throw me an underhanded compliment, filled with just enough spite and hostility to rain on my parade. But then, through the most seemingly loving—but really passive-aggressive—apologies I have ever received, we would end up back as "best friends," pretending to move forward—until the next jab was thrown. All sense of safety went out the window. At least with my friends in high school and college, I knew when the next insult was coming, but with these high-functioning postcollege grads I never knew when I was going to be iced out of a friendship.

Don't get me wrong. I played my part in all these friendships because they were all parts of me. It's not the easiest thing to admit, but it was true. Until I learned how to be fully me, without apology, I didn't experience true friendships. And

I love having girlfriends. Nothing is more remarkable than a good female friend. Yet so many of us stay connected to people who are not invested in creating healthy, loving relationships. Some of us are stuck in friendships that eat off the Language of Fat, thus spinning us into cycles of isolation, insecurity, and identity loss. It is up to us to seek out friendships with people who are kind, strong, honest, and supportive. But the only way to do that is to be kind to yourself first.

> *A friend is one who walks in when others walk out. —Walter Winchell*

Saboteurs v. Supporters

You have a choice to welcome either saboteurs or supporters into your life. Your sabotaging friendships usually involve some level of the Language of Fat, as that is the most unifying language that women are taught to speak together. The wreckage caused by saboteurs results in isolation, rejection, competition, jealousy, and insecurity. Supportive friendships, on the other hand, are much simpler. You feel better about yourself when you are with supporting friends. Your level of self-criticism and self-loathing decreases in direct proportion to the time you spend with this kind of friend.

If your life is overwhelmed with saboteurs, then you need to take a hard look at how and why you form these types of friendships. What is it saying about how you feel about yourself? The people you have in your life are mirrors for your personal and cultural beliefs. They are the mirrors of your real personality traits and a reflection of how you treat your friends.

?? Who Do You Know? ? ? ? ? ? ? ? ? ? ? ? ? ? ? ?

Take this quiz to see if you have more saboteurs or supporters in your life.

1. You show up to a party feeling fantastic in your new outfit. Your best friend says to you:

    a. "You look amazing! Can I borrow that shirt sometime?"

    b. "I didn't know they made that in your size."

    c. "Why are you so dressed up? Who are you trying to impress?"

    d. "Great, now I look horrible and underdressed next to you."

2. You are meeting your friend for dinner. When it comes time to order, she says:

    a. "This place looks yummy; I can't wait to eat a great meal."

    b. "I didn't know you could eat that. Aren't you still on your diet?"

    c. "Oh, I feel so fat, I shouldn't eat, really. Wanna share something?"

    d. "If I had your body, I'd order that too!"

3. You can't wait to tell your friend about the amazing man you've just started dating. She responds:

    a. "Great! It's about time someone saw how wonderful you are. You deserve it!"

    b. "Oh, I've heard about him. I heard that he's had a ton of girlfriends. Be careful."

c. "Do you think he can set me up with a friend of his?"

d. "You are so lucky. I'll never find a boyfriend—look at me!"

4. You tell your girlfriend something deeply private and personal. She:

   a. Takes it to the grave.

   b. Tells every one of your friends but makes them swear not to say anything.

   c. Brings it up when you are in a fight.

   d. Makes light of it, and then tells you her deeply private story that she thinks is worse.

5. You are enjoying a girls' day out at the movies with your friend. The guy standing in front of you at the snack counter is adorable. Your friend:

   a. Pays no attention. She is out with her best friend and fully in the moment!

   b. Flirts mercilessly with him, even though she's married.

   c. Pushes you to go up and talk to him, making a scene and embarrassing you.

   d. Can't keep eye contact with you because she is distracted by trying to make eye contact with him.

Any answers other than "a" mean your friend may be a saboteur.

SAB•O•TEUR \să-bə-tər\ *n* [F, fr. *saboter*] (1921) **1**: Can appear to be doing things in your favor when really she is about serving herself. **2**: Sometimes she can seem like a more exciting friend. **3**: Sometimes you choose the saboteur because you haven't learned any other way to be in a friendship with a woman. **4**: Sometimes you pick the saboteur because she seems the most safe. **5**: Saboteurs don't push you to stretch, challenge you to grow, or support you to change.

Take Five Minutes to Ask Yourself . . .

Do you feel like you surround yourself with body haters or chronic dieters? Do you feel your focus shift externally when you are around your female friends? Do you spend an excessive amount of your time with friends discussing food, fat, and weight?

What kind of friendships do you have? Do you laugh a lot? Are your friends loyal? Do you share common interests with them?

Figure out why you are attracted to your friends. Do you know what you value in your friendships? Have you ever truly thought about it?

The statistics on sanity are that one out of every four Americans is suffering from some form of mental illness. Think of your three best friends. If they are okay, then it's you.
—Rita Mae Brown

Beauty Is Only Skin Deep

There is nothing worse than standing next to your super-beautiful best friend as she bellows on about how ugly she is. A typical reaction is to begin to cut yourself down as well, so that you are both feeling miserable together. Or you say nothing and think to yourself, "Well, if she thinks she's ugly, then she must think I'm hideous!" Many of us don't even realize that interactions like this not only screw up our self-esteem but can ultimately destroy our friendships.

Jealousy and competitiveness are two very natural emotions you feel within friendships, but they are no doubt made worse by our society. The media makes a lot of money (as we have discussed) selling the notion that there can be only one "perfect woman," and that all women should be striving for that title. Current messaging tells women that they have to be in competition about their bodies and their romantic relationships—as if there is a limited supply of happiness, success, and contentment to go around.

Dear Jess,

Plain and simple: All of my friends are gorgeous and I am . . . not. I know that I'm not ugly by any means, but I am definitely not as hot as the rest of my group of friends, and I get reminders of that all the time. Guys hit on them constantly (there are four of us), and they get free drinks wherever we go. I swear, even people in clothing stores treat them differently by doting on them and asking them about their jewelry. How can I feel good about myself when I am hanging out with these goddesses?

Thanks, Shireen

Listen, I know that those considered pretty and attractive by cultural standards receive some preferential treatment. I won't argue that they probably get free drinks and more attention from men. I am certain they are getting special treatment in stores, especially if they show signs of being wealthy, as that is what stores are all about—selling things! But those are just surface qualities. It's time to get honest about your relationships and start standing up for yourself.

You have to feel good about yourself before you get into any friendship or relationship. When you allow your self-love to be determined by how many free drinks you get offered or who is hitting on you, then you are always going to come up empty. There will always be someone prettier or thinner or better dressed than you. If one of those girls happens to be in your group of friends, you have to be clear on what you get out of that relationship. What's more, your jealousy and judgment could be clouding some really fun moments with your friends.

Recognize social behaviors for what they are—you live in a society that values money, beauty, and body size above all else. If you want to spend your time chasing those ideals, you can. But even if you one day end up wealthy, beautiful, and thin, you will still have to deal with the human emotions involved in being friends with other people.

Friendship Checklist

Which of these characteristics do you look for in a friend?

- ■ Rich
- ■ Physically beautiful
- ■ Fashionable
- ■ Funny
- ■ Trustworthy

- Honest
- Interested in the same things as me
- Successful
- The same physical size as me
- Unique
- Critical
- Supportive
- Socially connected
- Smart
- Loving
- Empowered
- Generous

The qualities that you identify as being important to you will also tell you a lot about how you see yourself. Was there a nice mix of qualities, or were all of them pointing in one area?

What Does Friendship Mean to You?

Sometimes your friendships are formed intuitively because you just feel good being around people. Take it one step further and try to identify the emotions behind what you are receiving and giving in your friendships. That way you can better identify in the future if your friendships continue to serve you and your needs.

People come into our lives for many reasons. Some are to teach us great lessons over a long period of time, and some are to be but a moment's influence. The only thing that stays the same throughout your friendships is you. So if you are being clear, and the best version of yourself, then you have all you need on your end. You can't control why friends betray you or when they will. But you can control the way you feel about it.

Dear Jess,

I have been best friends with a woman named Colleen for twelve years. We have been through so much, college graduations and the births of our children. We were thick as thieves, but slowly something has been changing. Recently I lost a little bit of weight, and she has been treating me differently. When things are going really well in my life, she can barely muster up an encouraging word, but if I have a bad body day and I say something like, "Oh, I ate too much today" or "God, I feel so bloated," then she will chime in and jump on board and offer something in the conversation. It is almost as if she likes me better when I am sad. Could it really be about my losing weight?

—Jane

There are a lot of reasons why friendships change. Sometimes jealousy can be at the root of a friendship falling apart. Some people feel more comfortable when you are self-loathing or speaking the Language of Fat. Perhaps they are going through something that is hard to articulate, so they find it easier to use negative body talk. Or maybe they are just more content when you are not feeling as good in your own life. That doesn't mean they are evil, just uncomfortable in their own skin.

Sometimes there can be an unspoken body competition between friends that gets activated when one friend starts losing weight. Sit down with your friend about issues as soon as they arise. Don't wait for them to fester and bubble into more anger or distance. If this doesn't work, you may need to distance yourself from this friendship until you are getting what you deserve: a friend who is able to support you in all the experiences you are facing, both good and bad, at all times, and regardless of your body shape and size.

Girl Talk

- Don't engage in debates in which a woman is trying to talk you into acknowledging how much cellulite she has. Doesn't that sound ridiculous to you? What else can you be doing with your time? When you hear your friend say something damaging about herself, don't ignore it or compliment it away. Simply tell her, "I don't like to speak the Language of Fat. If you want to talk about how you are feeling or what you are struggling with today, I will listen, but I am not going to sit and talk about how fat you are." Find your version of those words and be strong and swift.

- Do you and your friends spend time bonding by going on diets together and talking about BOTOX? Try to figure out what else is missing in your lives. Are you unhappy in your careers? Are your romantic relationships really satisfying? Or do you forge bonds of friendship over such items as your weight, your diet techniques, or your desire for surgery?

- Take inventory of how you feel after each of your encounters. If you find that your body-loathing rises after you get together with your friends, take note. If you find that most of the conversation is consumed by talk of weight loss and BOTOX, take note. Point it out to them next time you all hang out.

Rarely does anyone challenge women to *not* speak the Language of Fat when they get together. It is almost expected. Get a group of women together, and what do they talk about? Odds are, their bodies. Even the most educated, most powerful, most successful women I know can be leveled into a pile of insecurity and paranoia by speaking the Language of Fat. On a personal level you can take each opportunity as it arises to challenge the Language of Fat.

> *Friendship is unnecessary, like philosophy, like art. . . . It has no survival value; rather it is one of those things that give value to survival. —C. S. Lewis*

Just Do It

Standing up to a friend or to a group of girlfriends can be scary. But ask yourself: Is it scarier than spending decades reinforcing negative body image thoughts, language, and action? Is it scarier than feeling depressed or less than fulfilled in relationships? Is it scarier than feeling the longing for a deeper friendship connection?

Removing yourself from the situation or defending yourself in the moment is one way to take care of you. In the end, though, you need to figure out for yourself how you contribute to the Language of Fat, and make a commitment to reject it as a bonding ritual. The friendships that are born out of this newfound strength and conviction will be much more rewarding in the long run. It takes a brave soul to look at the unhealthy bonding women do and choose not to be a part of it.

If you judge people, you have no time to love them. —Mother Teresa

How to Help

So what do you do when you see a friend who's in great danger but is unwilling to get help? The best way I know to answer that question is by enforcing the concept of walking your talk.

- In friendships it is important to remember that you are a mirror for the other person. If you want your friend to act with more self-care and self-respect, then make sure you are modeling those behaviors in yourself. If you want your friend to be faithful and trustworthy, then you, too, must have those qualities.
- Taking action may mean listening more than you talk, being firm and honest, and standing by your friend's side, loving her unconditionally.
- Being a friend of action means having patience and knowing that your friend will begin to help herself when she is ready. You can help her get the tools; you can even demonstrate how to use them, but until your friend is ready to pick up a tool herself, you will just have to be patient and wait for her to take action.

Walk Your Talk

I met two friends recently who demonstrated to me the true power of friendship and what it means to take a risk for someone you love.

Jenn and Nina had been friends for years and decided to

become roommates when they both moved to the same city after college. Soon after they moved in together, Jenn began hearing Nina throwing up in the bathroom, and she noticed that her friend was dieting and exercising excessively. Nina's health rapidly deteriorated. Jenn didn't know what to do, because every attempt she made to talk to Nina about her behavior was met with anger, resentment, and the silent treatment. Jenn felt like she was losing her good friend and found herself dealing with the hardest question in the friendship handbook: How do you talk to a friend who is not ready to listen? The answer: You can't.

I was not surprised that Nina greeted Jenn's offer to talk with hostility and punishment. She was clearly in denial and scared to death of letting her eating disorder go. It was her way of coping. Once this kind of destructive behavior takes a grip on your life, releasing it feels devastating. There is a false sense of safety within the disorder. Friends and family members need to remember that the logic with which we assess the situation is not at all logic that can be found within the person who is suffering.

As a friend you want to fight the disorder itself, to rationally debate its way of thinking or controlling. Unfortunately, that is a fight you will lose. It is not your job as a friend to fix or heal. But that doesn't mean you have to sit by and idly watch. You can do a number of things. You can try again to have a conversation about your feelings, not about the disorder. Tell your friend that you feel helpless. That you can see she is struggling both emotionally and physically and that you want to help her. Ask if there is something you can do. Oftentimes, as friends, we intervene instead of ask. See if by asking you can open up the door for your friend to tell you what she needs.

Other Strategies to Help Friends in Need

- Try to abstain from speaking the Language of Fat with your friend, even if she opens up and wants to talk about fat grams and calories. Make sure you steer the conversation back to feelings and emotions—even if you simply say, "I am not comfortable talking about this with you," or "I know that the food and weight are just symptoms of something greater. Do you want to talk about how you are feeling?"

- Try not to focus on the food she is eating or not eating. Try not to monitor her bathroom visits. She needs to feel she can trust you. Remember, she is not getting better for you or her family. She has to get better for herself.

- Make sure you also take care of your needs. Take time for yourself to experience things that make you feel strong and sound as a person. A friend who tries to be a martyr is not a helpful friend. You can best walk your talk by being loving and balanced.

I wish there were a quick and easy answer to "How do I help a friend?" but there isn't. You just have to continue to invest in that friendship and do the very best you can.

Friends Make All the Difference

One day, about nine months after corresponding via e-mail with Jenn, I was on a speaking tour and stopped at a residential treatment facility that specializes in eating disorders and body image issues. I was speaking to a group of patients, all of whom were hanging on for dear life.

As I finished up my talk, a woman approached me. "Hi, my name is Nina," she said. "You spoke to my roommate, Jenn, a while back. She wrote you an e-mail about my bulimia and binge eating.

"You helped her a lot," she continued. "I was defensive and hard to convince, but she never let up on me and always told me that she would fight it with me and that she believed I could get better. I had to move out for a few months because I hit bottom, but she never gave up on me and always asked me what she could do for me. I had no idea what to tell her, but that didn't matter. She didn't give up.

"I entered treatment here about a month ago, and when I heard you were coming, I sent her an e-mail. She wanted you to know that she walked her talk. It worked. She is the reason I am here."

Then she corrected herself. "Actually, I'm the reason I am here. But having a friend like Jenn makes all the difference in the world."

And there it was. Another testament to what happens when people take a risk for someone they love.

It takes a long time to grow an old friend.
—John Leonard

TAKE ACTION

1. Remember that you don't have to use the Language of Fat to bond in your friendships. And when you hear your friend using this language, you can speak up and say something.

2. Take an inventory of your friendships. Do you surround yourself with saboteurs or supporters?

3. The people you attract into your life as friends serve as mirrors for your beliefs and thoughts. Get clear on what you'd like to give and get in a relationship. (See checklist pages 136–137.)

4. If you are involved in a toxic friendship, you can get out of it. Be willing to take a risk on your own behalf. Can you disappoint another to be true to yourself?

5. The best way to help a friend is to walk your talk.

6. Never give up on yourself or your friendships. Strive to create relationships with people who treat you with the respect, love, and kindness you deserve!

Chapter Nine

"I'm So Gross—I Have Nothing to Wear!"

Most commonly heard:
In closets, dressing rooms, and bedrooms nationwide.

Translation(s):
Can mean any of the following, but is not limited to:

"I am trying to impress someone and I feel nervous and insecure."

"I feel inadequate as a woman because I don't have the stylish clothes I see in magazines!"

"I equate my self-worth with my clothing size."

It's Time to Come Out of the Closet

Something vaguely resembling a Greek tragedy takes place every time I go into my closet to get dressed. I wish I could say I'm being melodramatic, but I'm not. "What should I wear today?" Five simple words, for some. For me it's a moral dilemma, and the consequences can have epic proportions.

Haunted by the memories of past fashion disasters, I take small, careful steps into enemy territory and open my closet door. I know the terrain. I have studied it for years. I have the

147

same strategy, the same plan. Get in and get out. As fast as I can. Don't look at myself naked in the mirror. Don't stop to ponder, poke, or pick. Just dodge in, grab something resembling an outfit, and get out as quickly as possible.

When it's over, I stop to survey the spoils of my war. Oh, no. I'm not happy with my outfit. I must venture in again, go behind enemy lines, and wage another attack.

This time I emerge victorious. I have found an outfit that will surely cover, hide, and protect my assets when, lo and behold, I discover a lone stain undetected by the dry cleaners, or a snug-fitting waistline that I could have sworn fit fine a few days ago. Or I'm faced with an outdated, trying-too-hard, doesn't-really-fit-my-body shirt that I bought because it was on sale.

As I stand wrapped in the cloak of my valiant battle, I am ashamed, angry, embarrassed, and hopeless. I experience such a swelling of emotion that I find I must bellow at the world around me, at the injustice in my life, a scream so loud and so soul-shaking that it most definitely wakes up the neighbors: "Why, oh why, am I so gross that I have nothing to wear?"

No matter that the two phrases making up this sentence don't really connect.

"I feel gross" signals an immersion in the Language of Fat, really covering up some deeply rooted body-loathing and an inability to express other emotions, such as anxiety, joy, trepidation, and so on. "I have nothing to wear" signals that I am at the end of my stylish rope with nontrendy clothing that may or may not actually fit my current body size. Apart, these phrases only pack a small punch. But put them together and you have a supersize version of self-loathing.

Understanding the Closet Meltdown

All logic goes out the window when you're staring straight ahead at the insides of your closet. Thousands of dollars worth of shiny, soft, smooth material we call clothing—and still we are certain we have nothing to wear. And that we are gross. And fat. And undesirable. And ugly. What is it that brings us to the brink of emotional and spiritual despair when we open up our closet doors? What moves us to swear on our grandmother's grave that we will get back into our skinny jeans before the summer is over?

Though the journey has been long, I refuse to any longer be a woman who mangles her body to fit into clothes. What happened to the sweet notion of finding clothes that just fit your body? Whose militaristic idea was it to have you mentally manipulated around a small piece of fabric, a label carrying a number, haphazardly sewn into the back of your pants?

As if chronic dieting didn't have us already withdrawn from our potential and power, our society's drive to buy and consume clothing that will make us look like the "perfect woman" sends us into an ego-crushing downward spiral and an agony-filled existence. It replaces bigger topics—like, for instance, world events or social issues. Instead, across the country each morning, women are often more concerned with which jeans make our butts look small.

Sometimes I think it's a conspiracy of sorts. Or some kind of mind control. How else can you explain the behavior at the half yearly sale at your favorite department store? Barbarian aggression is on full display when women groan, gruff, and sometimes jab elbows at each other, hoping to find that marked-down item that we wouldn't normally pay more than ten bucks for, but since it's in a bin identified with a big red sign that says SALE, we will pay whatever it costs and declare it a steal!

Who are you when you give up all hope and faith in the world because you can't find a cute pair of shoes to match your outfit? Where do you go when you launch missiles at your fragile bits of self-worth while standing in front of a dressing room mirror in a bathing suit?

Make no mistake, there is a tragedy playing out. And you are at war with an enemy so imbedded in our consumer culture that you are sometimes oblivious to the battle. This war is waged at home, each and every morning, each and every time you go to open that closet door and get dressed.

Are you with me?

"Women's fashion" is a euphemism for fashion created by men for women. —Andrea Dworkin

---

Fashion Is King

Even when I was a little girl, I knew exactly how I felt about clothes: I loved them! I had my favorite T-shirt (cowgirl riding a horse), and I wasn't afraid to tell whoever was in charge of dressing me exactly what I wanted to wear. I knew instinctively as I grew older what I wanted to put on my body, and it was usually determined by what felt good. Cotton, good. Polyester, bad. And for a while it was that simple . . . comfort was king. Then I hit those invariably rough preteen years, and my attitude toward clothing changed completely.

I had already started to dislike my body at eleven and was

dieting regularly by twelve, and so by the time the fashion-conscious years of thirteen and fourteen came around, I identified clothes as a dire necessity that impacted my everyday existence as a teenager. I saw clothes in two shades: those that fit and those that didn't. And so I began my love affair with sizing and numbers before I had even mastered long division.

I became attached to the sizes of clothing that other people wore; studying their shapes, guessing what size was printed on their jeans labels. I became a pop culture connoisseur of fashion trends, running out to buy gummy bracelets, jelly shoes, neon prints, and mesh tops.

Even in all of my body consciousness I was realistically aware that I didn't possess the long, lean legs that made the hottest jeans look so good on the models. I knew that though other girls could get away with not wearing bras under their shirts, I had to find clothing that was made for a girl with boobs. I knew how to dress my young curves, and I would spend hours in front of the mirror at night trying on different combinations. I lived for my friends' declarations each morning at school. "Cute outfit!" It was almost as addictive as hearing "You've lost weight!"

But no matter how creative I got and no matter how hard I tried to stay current, it seemed like I could never stay on top of the trends for long. There would always be some girl who had a cuter purse, or some fad that started just as I was stockpiling last season's look. I didn't understand that the fashion for my youth was being driven by a larger industry, one that made a boatload of money on girls like me trying so hard to keep up with the times.

The deeper I got into my love of fashion and the more

curves I developed, the harder it became to shop for "girly" clothes. I found myself at the larger end of the junior section before I faced the fact that I had to look in the "misses" department. Then a miracle would happen (well, a diet miracle, anyway) and I would shed a few pounds and find myself back in juniors. The bouncing I did between the worlds of juniors and misses was actually a larger metaphor for my entire relationship with being a woman. I was in constant flux about where I wanted to be in life—a little girl or a growing woman.

Clothing Is an Emotional Costume

Clothing projects how you feel about yourself, your body, your relationships, your dreams and desires. You dress for success, for love, for friendship, to impress, to alienate, to rebel, to intimidate, to seduce, to fool, to bond, and to make a statement.

And yet how many of you are afraid to go into your closets? Do you behave as if the small sliver of space where you hang your clothes is the ultimate keeper of your demons? For some it is. For others, it chronicles all of the breakups and breakthroughs of life.

Dear Jess,

My closet is the dark side. Sometimes I don't even want to walk around near it. If I am lying on my bed and the closet doors are open, I have to get up and close them. I don't want to be reminded of what lives inside. Nothing but old sizes I can't fit into. One day I went to try on an old pair of jean cutoffs that I haven't worn since I was twenty-two (I am twenty-nine now), and my thighs looked like ham hocks in them. I couldn't even close the top button. I just sat there and cried. Actually, I didn't even sit, because I couldn't. I couldn't even bend my legs to sit down because my legs were losing circulation. I look at an entire closet filled with expensive clothes and think that I am so fat and I have nothing nice to wear. This is mortifying to me. It pains me to share this, but what can I do?

—Sarah

Here is the truth: Our bodies change! For good or bad, they do. Your body won't look exactly the way it did at eighteen, and while it doesn't mean that you aren't allowed to be concerned if you think you've gotten out of shape or something, it does mean that you can stop trying to step back into seven-year-old wardrobe options and expect the same results. Would you want to go back and date the boyfriend you had at eighteen? (Not me!) Try to look at your clothing the same way: It's served its purpose, but for you to still try to hold on to it tells me you are not focusing on who you are today. You can't go back to old clothing to try to relive some past experience. None of us can be physically frozen in time. We are living, evolving beings.

Spring Cleaning: Four Easy Steps to a Better You

1. Remove from your closet all of the "old sizes" that you can't fit into.

2. Fill up your closet instead with clothes that fit you now. If you have held on to anything for longer than a year, thinking you are going to one day get back into it—get rid of it. It is like having pictures of old boyfriends around after you are married. You can go back and relive the old times all you want, but the fact is you are now with someone else, and keeping those photos around will only cause you pain in the end.

3. Your closet can be a light-filled space that reflects how you feel about yourself now. It can be filled with positive reality, instead of outdated old illusions.

4. Remember, clothes are just pieces of fabric—they hold as much power over your life as you let them. Savor the memories from wearing those old clothes and what they represented for you in the past, record the moments in your journal if you have to, but get rid of the clothes that don't fit, and do the same thing about the expectations on your body.

You're Already in Your Real Body

Dear Jess,

I have been on diets my entire life, so I am rarely the same size for very long. My closet is filled with a lot of different clothes from various times of my dieting life. I can fluctuate as many as ten sizes! I am particularly obsessed with fitting into a pair of pants that I was able to wear in high school and college. I keep them around to remind me of my "thin days," but they depress me more than they inspire me lately. I am afraid to stop dieting because I don't want to balloon any more than I already am. Truth is, I probably don't even know what size I truly am. I don't think I've seen my real body in years and years.

—Margaret

The attachment to needing to wear a certain size is similar to the attachment to being a certain weight. It is limiting and random and pointless. Everyone's body is different and unique. The twists, turns, dimples, dents, and wrinkles vary for everyone. Yet on some strange level you are all striving to be the same size—and that size is whatever you deem to be "skinny" enough. For some it is a zero. For others a fourteen. And there is incredible pressure on women to buy into this sliding scale of self-worth. No one's life ended because they couldn't fit into last year's jeans. But many people's lives have ended in the pursuit of that perfect elusive weight and size, the number that seems like it would solve all of our problems.

Margaret said she hadn't seen her real body in years. Think about that. What body is she walking around in? A body punished and restricted from being nourished? A body hiding and sulking through overindulgence? A body berating itself for being a failure? Where is her true body? Where is yours? It is the body you have right now, regardless of size and shape. It is the skin you are in today—not tomorrow.

Size Is an Arbitrary Number

Believe it or not, sizing depends on where certain clothes are manufactured and how the manufacturer wishes to market the line. Have you noticed that when shopping for extremely expensive brands, you may find yourself in a smaller size? That is because some companies wish to capitalize on the mental warfare that is associated with women's sizing. They know that women are socialized to want to be the smallest size possible, and if they can get you thinking that your $1,500 just bought you a better feeling about yourself, then they think you will come back and spend more—just so you can feel good about your size.

Style Secrets

You know what my style secret truly is? I find clothes that fit my body properly. No matter what the size says. Even if you have to buy two different sizes, get your head in the game to find the best fit, not a certain size, because clothing is not a perfect science—people still make clothing, and people are still fallible. Patterns can be cut differently, and two of the same size pants can fit very differently. So try on multiple sizes till you find the one that works for your body. Dress for your age and be realistic about your shape. Just because a style is in for a prepubescent girl doesn't mean it will translate well on an older woman. Get a reality check on what truly does look best on you. If you aren't sure, grab the most honest group of friends you have and ask them.

All women face a challenge in finding clothing that works on their bodies. Your body is brilliantly unique. It may take more patience than you have sometimes, but learning to dress your body for who you are today can help alleviate an overstuffed closet full of clothing memories and reminders of failed diet plans. Most of all, feel good in your skin, because a genuine glow of self-esteem is the sexiest accessory anyone can have.

> *I base most of my fashion sense on what doesn't itch. —Gilda Radner*

The Closet Monster

Dear Jess,

Please help my girlfriend! I think the "closet monster" has gotten her. She literally cannot get dressed without asking me twenty million times if she looks fat. Not only that, but she will ask me if "this goes together." I am a guy and have no idea, so I always tell her yes. She sometimes cries when she gets dressed, and we are always twenty minutes late to everything because she is busy in the bathroom checking her outfit in a "different light." I swear, I wish I was making this up, but I am not. I have no idea how she got this way. She wasn't like this when we started dating—but she needs help now for sure.

—Bryan

> *Clothes make the man. Naked people have little or no influence on society. —Mark Twain*

A Guy's Guide to Closet Meltdowns

Unfortunately, when you are a bystander, there is no sure-fire plan to escape someone's closet meltdown. Here are some simple tips for staying safe in this war zone.

- **Don't** just write it off as hormones or PMS.

- **Don't** try to smooth things over by saying, "But I think you are beautiful."

- **Don't** scream, "Get your butt moving, we're gonna be late!"

- **Don't** point at the jam-packed closet full of clothes as a reminder that she does indeed have something to wear.

- **Don't** try to reason with the voices in her head.

- **Don't** take it personally.

- By all means, **do not** ignore the meltdown. Benign neglect doesn't work here.

- **Don't** try to offer up fashion advice unless you really know what you are talking about.

- **Don't** use self-deprecating jokes about how "fat" *you* are.

- **Do** ask her if there is anything you can do for her right now.

- **Do** go up to her and gently put a hand on her back. The touch of a loving friend or partner actually can ground her freak-out energy.

- **Do** speak calmly and in feeling words.

- **Do** let her know you care for her and are sorry to see her feeling like this.

- **Do** offer to sit and talk about what's really going on with her.

- **Do** remember that you can't fix her. Remind her (gently!) that she'll have to emerge from the pile of clothes sometime—right?

Stay Out of the Danger Zone

Unless you're going to live in a nudist colony, clothing and body image will continue to be a force in your life. No matter whether you are a high-end fashionista or fancy yourself a thrift-store diva, what you choose to wear expresses how you feel about yourself—more specifically, how you feel about your body. There are ways to combat the incessant neuroticism and self-critique that our culture places on us about our bodies and our fashion. In the same way that you are decoding the Language of Fat and trying to find replacements for all of the words that you use that are hazardous to your health, so too must you straighten out your beliefs about your body, your size, and the clothes you choose to wear.

For me the days of my Greek tragedies are over. When I am the slightest bit tempted to believe that I am not a worthy human being because I can't find a top to match my pants, I now know that I am in a danger zone with the Language of Fat, and it is a cue for an emotional time-out.

Knowing and understanding the shape and size of my body and deciding how I like to dress my body empowers me. I have learned to avoid the marketing trap of being a certain size and the closet meltdowns with people I love. It took some work for me to get this way. I eventually got very good at creating a new kind of theatrics for myself in the morning. And this one has a theme of love and acceptance. There is no substitute for self-love. No quick fix, no shortcut, and no certain size or style that can replace it. If you are not currently practicing it, then you must begin somewhere. These are all merely suggestions. But they worked for me, a retired actress in the Greek closet tragedies. And I know they can work for you, too.

How to Make Love in the Morning . . . to Yourself

1. Take three extra minutes before you rush out of bed, and really pay attention to your body. Listen to it, feel every ache and pain, nervous twitter, or heartbeat. Just listen to it.

2. Stand before your mirror naked before you get dressed, and really look at your body. Don't avoid it. Look at it as lovingly as you can, and while you do, take three deep breaths. Watch your belly rise and fall as your body begins to work for you!

   Note: I know this whole notion of looking at your body naked with the lights on and your eyes open may seem like torture rather than a healing technique, but bear with me—you can work your way up to this step.

3. Before entering your closet, close your eyes and ask yourself what you feel like wearing. Ask your body what it needs. Listen to the first gut instinct you have. Maybe today your body needs you in an elastic waist versus a tight belt, or you're really leaning toward purple instead of slate gray. Whatever it is, trust your gut and choose accordingly.

4. If you find yourself going into a tailspin and feeling edgy, agitated, or unhappy, stop whatever you are doing. Hang the clothes back up. And repeat steps 2 and 3.

TAKE ACTION

1. Throw out all notions of what clothing size you *should* be. Instead, focus on how your body *feels* in clothing.

2. Become more realistic about your true shape. Seek to find clothing that really fits your body well. Don't be afraid to buy a different size.

3. Remember, all women have issues finding clothes that fit. Dump the "grass is always greener" attitude and work with your body to find clothes that actually fit.

4. Recognize the Language of Fat that is present during closet meltdowns.

5. Remember that your worth does not hinge on what you are wearing today.

6. Raise your voice. Write to fashion magazines, clothing stores, and designers, and let them know what you think about their marketing, their clothing, and their availability to women of all shapes and sizes.

7. Learn how to make love in the morning to yourself! Practice self-love and kindness with your body before you get dressed. You'll notice the difference. I promise.

Chapter Ten

"But I'm Just Trying to Be Healthy!"

Most commonly heard:

In the mind-set of someone who is compulsively searching for the magic bullet that will suddenly make her thin, toned, and . . . happy!

Also found in the excuses for our strange dieting rituals, which for some reason usually start on a Monday.

Translation(s):

Can mean any of the following, but is not limited to:

"I want desperately to believe that my punishing way of restricting and obsessing is somehow good for me and what I need to do in order to really achieve my goals."

"I have no idea what healthy really means for me, but it's kind of trendy right now, so I'll say it."

"Well, God knows I don't want to be *fat*, so I must do whatever it takes, right?"

Stop the Madness

Raise your hand if you have ever been on a diet. I don't know one woman in my personal or professional life who hasn't tried to lose weight at some point in her lifetime. Not one. And I mean women of all shapes and sizes. It doesn't matter whether they technically could afford to shed pounds or not. I simply do not know one woman who has not tried a diet of some kind.

I'm not talking about a "lifestyle change" or a food modification for true physical health reasons. I am talking about a good ol' "get down to the nitty gritty I wanna lose weight for cosmetic and vanity reasons only and I will do all sorts of strange things to achieve weight loss" kind of diet.

You follow?

Some women pass on dieting tips as easily as they say hello and good-bye. Some families pass down diet tips from generation to generation. And most women—okay, all women I know—voraciously read or watch TV to find the newest, most surefire diet tip that will finally answer the question, "If I keep dieting so much, why can't I keep the weight off?"

The answer to that question is—because you diet.

Dieting teaches you nothing but shame, blame, restriction, and guilt.

And I should know. If they gave out awards for dieting, I'd have a whole shelf lined with them. I have been on all of them, in some form or another. I used to be a walking encyclopedia of fat grams, calories, and carbs. I didn't know how to create intimacy in my relationships, but I sure as heck knew how many calories were in a piece of pizza.

At the entry point of every single diet I embarked on, I used the phrase "But I'm just trying to be healthy." And it worked. When you say that to people, they back off. Because who in their right mind would want to stop you from being healthy? Only mean people and enemies. Not friends or family or people who truly love you. No, I could spray everyone with this emotional pepper spray and no one would come near me. And therefore no one could really discover that what I was doing to my body wasn't healthy at all.

Spending hours locked away in my room, using black Magic Marker to circle places on my thighs and upper arms, noting them as "problem areas," or working out four hours a day on less than four hundred calories and spitting out any excess water in my mouth into little plastic baggies. Or eating no meat, then no carbs of any kind, then no meat and no carbs, then no fruit, then no sugar, then no cooked foods, then no processed foods, until soon I was snacking on lettuce sandwiches and a lot of resentment.

?? "But I'm Being Healthy" Checklist ??????

Do you think being healthy means:

- Eating nothing with fat in it?
- Never having dessert?
- Eating no carbs?
- Being able to fit into the smallest size in the clothing store?
- Working out every day?
- Having physical beauty?
- Being popular?
- Being the weight the doctor's chart tells you to be?
- Having your mate think you're attractive?

Or do you think being healthy means:

■ Showing love freely and easily?

■ Being able to run a marathon?

■ Being able to walk a flight of stairs?

■ Being able to say no to people gracefully?

■ Being open to expressing emotions?

■ Letting go of control?

■ Taking time off for vacation or just playing?

■ Being a kind friend?

■ Having faith in a higher power or belief in the workings of the world?

■ Being a huge success?

■ Loving the skin you are in?

To Be or Not to Be Healthy

Who really knows what will make you healthy, anyway? You can go crazy trying to follow the latest health breakthroughs that seem to come out every fifteen minutes. Don't you know about the basic commonsense motto "All things in moderation"? Sounds good, doesn't it? But with a country that is getting heavier by the second, and with eating disorders and depression on a steady rise, what are you missing when it comes to thinking about your health?

Let me say up front, you won't solve this issue in one chapter. You probably won't solve this issue in one lifetime. Because to talk about health is to talk about more than just weight charts and fat counts. It is to talk about wholeness, wellness, and a sense of complete balance mentally, physically, emotionally, and spiritually. And there are a lot of people out there who make money off of us being unwell, confused, tortured, desperate, unhappy, and insecure. The diet and health industry makes billions and billions each year selling us "health."

Even the word "health" can be found in the Language of Fat as a big catchall phrase meaning something other than fat. Come on, let's face it: When people say they want to be healthy, they really mean they don't want to be fat. Because, as we discussed, the term "fat" carries a big charge for everyone. Most people see it as meaning that you are not all right, not happy, not accepted, and oftentimes not loved.

Now, please don't misunderstand. I am not saying you shouldn't be striving for health and longevity in your life. And I am not even saying that most people couldn't stand to adapt a more balanced way of eating, moving, and feeling through life. But I do believe, with the current state of affairs in the culture, and with so many women and men completely and utterly miserable with their bodies, starving themselves, beating up

What's Your Definition of Healthy?

- Is it starvation, restriction, intense discipline?
- Is it digesting all sorts of unpronounceable herbs and vitamins?
- Is it a number on a scale?
- Is it peace of mind?
- Or a well-rounded emotional outlook on life?

If you could create a working definition of what it means for you to be healthy in your own words, with your own understanding of your own goals, what would it be?

You can be the physically healthiest person out there, eating everything you are supposed to, working out consistently—and you might step off the curb and get hit by a bus. Maintaining your physical health is important so you can live longer, but if you aren't enjoying the life you're living, is it worth it?

their self-esteem, feeling depressed, and then gorging to cover up the feelings, that you have to reframe this dialogue about what is truly healthy and what isn't. And stop using this term as a slick marketing ploy to sell a product.

> *There's lots of people in this world who spend so much time watching their health that they haven't the time to enjoy it.* —Josh Billings

Happiness Does Not Begin on Monday

Diets always start on Mondays. Why is that? Mondays stink as it is. The first day back from the weekend. The slowest productivity day of the week. And yet Mondays are seen as the day of redemption. You always promise yourself to start fresh on Monday. "I will begin eating better on Monday." "I will begin exercising on Monday." "On Monday I will eat more vegetables." Next to New Year's Day, Monday is the most popular day to start your life over. But what about the other six days of the week? You can't begin to take care of yourself then? You have to wait till Monday? I never understood this. It puts an awful lot of pressure on Monday, don't you think?

"I'll start my diet on Monday" is part of the Language of Fat. It is from the damaged school of thought that says your life will begin when you are thinner, that miraculously all the issues in your life will clear up when you have a smaller body. Ironically, for some of us the thought of giving up dieting in our everyday life is frightening.

The Endless Quest for Perfection

Dear Jess,

I have heard you speak before about how bad diets are for you. But I don't feel like I would have any control over my life if I was not on a diet. I need that restriction to feel like I am working toward my goal weight. I try not to become too strict with myself, but I just can't imagine my life without being on a diet, since that is what I have been doing since I was twelve years old. I am now thirty-six. I don't think this is way out of line, to be careful about what you eat, because I am just trying to be healthy.

—Dana

Have you been dieting for well over half your life? Has the fact that you haven't been able to reach the size you desire masked any of the other accomplishments you have achieved in your life? Do you think you are a failure for not reaching your goal size? I wonder how many other areas of your life are not being honored because you are being so restrictive.

Dieting has become such an ingrained part of living your life that I can understand that changing that mentality would be scary. But can you honestly say you are happy with the way things are right now? Or do you feel like you are in this perpetual quest for something that you just can't achieve? That is the shame and blame that I believe the diet mentality teaches you. You aren't happy in the now. You are only happy when you restrict your eating by dieting. And that carries over into other areas of your life and into your general outlook on life, actually. Don't blame yourself; you may just want to change your goal.

It's time for the woman you are now to confront your inner dieting child and find out if this is a pattern you wish to continue in your life. Being healthy is about having a well-rounded life. Moving your body, eating balanced meals, and working on your emotional and spiritual health. If you spend all your time focused on food and your size, you may be missing the fullness of your life that is available to you now, not five pounds from now. Health comes in all shapes and sizes. There is no universal healthy weight—regardless of what your doctor's office weight charts tell you. You have to be responsible for what you put into your body and what you put into your mind. You have to be responsible for how you move your body and how you talk to your body. Some people find it challenging to accept their body any size larger than what they feel, by society's standards, it should be. That can be frustrating for the body-conscious, because you forget about this little thing called genetics. We can alter our features with surgery or extreme dieting, but in the end we can't change genetics. Simply put: Everyone comes in different shapes and sizes, some larger, some smaller.

Interesting fact: In 1920 women attained the right to vote. This was also the first year of the Miss America pageant.
—WAC Stats: The Facts About Women

Health Comes in All Sizes

Dear Jess,

I am a substantial woman. After I moved to this new city, I fell down while Rollerblading and sprained my wrist. When I was sitting in the ER, the doctor who was treating me said, "You know, you should think about losing a few pounds." Like it was any of his business! I came in for a sprained wrist, not gastric bypass surgery. So when I told him that I wasn't interested in losing weight, he looked at me like I was some kind of freak. He mentioned the risks of high blood pressure and cholesterol, and I kindly informed him of my prior test results. Shouldn't doctors and nurses know that health comes in all sizes?

Sincerely and substantially yours, Marissa

It isn't anyone's business to offer insight into your weight, unless you ask for that advice. Unfortunately, we live in a very fat-phobic society, where size discrimination is the last bastion of "acceptable" discrimination. People think that they have a perverse and profound right to comment on people's body shapes and sizes, especially in the medical profession. They may feel they are entitled to because they are more aware of all the health complications from carrying extra weight. But they have to look at people on a case-by-case basis and not jump to broad conclusions.

Health does come in all sizes. Just because you may be

larger or "substantial" doesn't mean that you are unhealthy at all! You have to also remember that doctors and nurses are just people who have formed their own belief systems around their bodies, and many of them also speak the Language of Fat. No one is impervious to this language.

> *I believe that every human has a finite*
> *number of heartbeats. I don't intend*
> *to waste any of mine running*
> *around doing exercises.*
> —Neil Armstrong

We Aren't Just What We Eat

You would never treat your friends the way you treat your body. You can be so disgustingly critical and harsh and punishing. And yet your body is always there for you—pulling you through another ridiculous week of eating only peanut butter and celery sticks. It is tempting when speaking of health to talk about food. For some people the topic of food is a safe and comforting one. This is also part of the Language of Fat, because there is more to being healthy than just what you are eating. Are you smoking? Having unprotected sex? Wearing your seat belt? Releasing your anger? Taking naps? All of these have the same impact on health as what we put in our mouths. But with all the talk in our country about obesity, our attention now more than ever is turned to weight and our food. And while it is important to some degree, it is not the biggest issue here.

Health Sanity Quiz ? ? ? ? ? ? ? ? ? ? ? ? ? ? ?

Are you overdoing it in your quest to be healthy? How much balance do you have in your physical and emotional life? Is your self-worth tied to how well you do on your diet or how many times you work out? Take the quick quiz below to gauge your health sanity.

1. When you miss a scheduled workout, do you:

    a. Freak out and jog everywhere for the rest of the day?

    b. Swear off eating until you can hit the treadmill?

    c. Get angry at yourself or feel like a failure?

    d. Forgive yourself and pick another day that week to go work out?

2. When you realize that you've gained ten pounds, do you:

    a. Call your doctor and schedule your gastric bypass surgery?

    b. Avoid your friends and family?

    c. Begin dieting immediately . . . or plan to on Monday?

    d. Not do anything drastic? Sometimes your weight will fluctuate. You will monitor your thoughts, feelings, and actions more closely to see if there is anything to adjust.

3. You don't feel that you are healthy if you:

    a. Are not at the weight you were at in high school.

    b. Are not working out every day.

    c. Are eating foods other than carrots and rice cakes.

    d. Are not spending time with family, friends, and yourself.

4. You believe that dieting is:

    a. A way of life; everyone should do it.

    b. Only for the strong and determined.

    c. The only way to maintain your figure.

    d. A medieval torture device that should be against the law.

5. You believe that health is:

    a. A number on the scale or a size on your pair of pants.

    b. Being able to run ten miles without stopping.

    c. Not having an ounce of fat on your body.

    d. A combination of balance of mind, body, and spirit.

If you answered anything but "d" to these questions, you may want to examine your attitudes toward "health."

Remember that a perfect body is really a body that is at peace with being imperfect. Health is a continuum, a process you strive to create in your everyday life. True success in health has to come from a well-rounded approach that takes into consideration real-life day-to-day happenings and interruptions. Being healthy is learning to love what you've got. Don't give your power away to diet plans, supplements, and magic pills that promise you an easy shortcut to a perfect body. It is alluring to believe that some product out there holds the key to your happiness, but it doesn't.

You can outdistance that which is running after you, but not what is running inside of you. —Rwandan proverb

Walk Your Talk

For a very long time I didn't love my body. I didn't have any appreciation for my body. It was something outside of me. A foreign object. Something I fought against, felt betrayed by, and was disappointed in.

Until one day I decided to run a marathon.

Yes, that's right. I wasn't at my "goal weight." I wasn't in perfect shape or running twenty-six miles a day. Nevertheless, the idea found me in a bathroom, of all places.

I was having lunch with a friend, and when I went to the bathroom of the restaurant, I looked up to see a sign staring at me. It was an advertisement for a program that trained people to run the Honolulu Marathon and raise money for people living with HIV/AIDS. At the bottom of the sign it said A WALK YOUR TALK PRODUCTION.

It was the last sentence that caught my eye. "Walk your talk" was a phrase that had been the foundation of my work for the previous ten years. It was the only piece of tried-and-true advice I could live by. On impulse I took a registration form and didn't tell a soul. Was I crazy? I was actually contemplating running a marathon! I thought about it day and night. *What if I'm too out of shape? I have never done this before. I don't run marathons. What if I can't finish it?* But the little sentence on the bottom of the pamphlet, right next to the "Walk Your Talk Production" part, said it all: "Come on, why don't you finish what you start?"

I was approaching ten years of recovery from the eating disorders and body hatred that had ruled my life as a young woman. Ten years of working on changing my thoughts and language. Now it was time to take action. Although I had a significant amount of recovery in my life, I still had fear that I wouldn't make it through an entire marathon. I had never relied on my body to serve me in such a capacity before. I didn't spend much time, if any, thinking about the amazing feats it performs every day just breathing, creating new cells, digesting, growing, living, or protecting me. Providing for me the vehicle in which I move through this world. And here I was, asking it to carry me twenty-six point two miles. My goal was not to win the race. It was merely to finish it. And in order to do that, I had to work *with* my body. Not against it. So I began training.

During the marathon, when I hit mile number twenty, I thought to myself, *Okay, I can stop now, I came pretty far, I can call it quits and still tell people I ran twenty miles*. Then I spotted someone who had finished the race. The person had a T-shirt on that I hadn't seen in any of the marathon gift stores. It said FINISHER.

At mile twenty-four I thought about quitting again. Even though I was so close, I didn't think I could make it through the pain and exhaustion I was feeling. It was easy for my mind to wander and think about how I used to push my body hours on the treadmill to burn off whatever I had eaten for lunch. And here I was pushing my body again, but this time for a different reason. Could my body tell the difference? Throughout the entire training process I'd had to feed my body, rest my body, and honor my body's aches and pains. I learned to listen to my body in a way I had never known possible. I had to show it patience, reverence, respect, and love. Or else it wouldn't take me the distance.

I don't remember much of the last two miles, but I do remember what it felt like as I approached the finish line. There were a handful of die-hard supporters cheering us on. I began to hallucinate. Ringing in my ears were all of the horrible things I used to say to myself when I spoke the Language of Fat.

But then I heard a different voice speaking in a new language. *You did it. In this body. In this skin. Right here. Right now. We are celebrating our health. We are working together. I am not betraying you. I will carry you across the line. We will achieve this together. We have finished.*

Eight hours and six minutes. My final time. I fell to the ground and cried. It was official. I had completed my first marathon. I had achieved the most memorable moment of my life. In addition to being chafed, sweaty, exhausted, and incredibly hungry, I was so damn proud. I had walked my talk and finished.

And I have the T-shirt to prove it.

I don't want to get to the end of my life and find that I lived just the length of it. I want to have lived the width of it as well.
—Diane Ackerman

TAKE ACTION

1. Dieting teaches you shame, blame, guilt, and more shame. Try to avoid it at all costs.

2. Take out your inventory book or journal and spend time writing down what the word "healthy" means to you. Begin by writing your first instinct and then allow your mind to expand to all possible definitions of health. Refer to the "But I'm Being Healthy" Checklist to help you get started. (See pages 165-166.)

3. Keep it in perspective. Your pursuit of health and wellness shouldn't get in the way of your friendships and relationships. True health blends easily into all areas of your life.

4. Remember that you don't have to punish your body in order to be healthy. If your health regimen is making you feel forced, restricted, sad, depressed, or frustrated, reconsider your goals and the way you are reaching them.

5. Keep in mind that there is a huge industry dedicated to selling you health in quick fixes and promises. Be smart and savvy about the messaging coming your way regarding what it means to be healthy.

6. Health can come in various shapes and sizes. Open your mind and watch your language!

7. Treat your body like you would treat a friend. Work with your body to move it, feed it balanced meals, and speak lovingly about it.

Chapter Eleven

"Are You Sure This Doesn't Make My Butt Look Big?"

Most commonly heard:
Floating around in the heads of those trying to shake years of body-loathing and speaking the Language of Fat.

Translation(s):
Can mean any of the following, but is not limited to:

"I don't feel comfortable yet letting go of the Language of Fat, so I hold on to these insecurities that make me feel more in control."

"I'm trying not to speak the Language of Fat, but it is so hard when everyone around me does."

"I am still trying to fit in and blend because feeling good about yourself is not a common thing people bond over."

Please Put Down the Ice Cream!

I had just spent four hours talking my girlfriend out of eating a gallon of ice cream, calling her ex-boyfriend, and signing up for an online diet club. Her breakdown was brought on by this aforementioned ex showing up at her best friend's birthday party with a new girlfriend. Their relationship had been over just a month, and so technically he was violating the cooling period by bringing out a new flame and introducing her around as his new girlfriend. My friend was devastated. But none of her other friends were surprised, because he had never treated her with the respect we thought she deserved.

She felt betrayed. Humiliated. Sad. Lonely. And rejected. All the perfect triggers to begin speaking the Language of Fat. And that is exactly what she did.

"But, Jess, you don't understand. He loved me. At least I thought he did. Maybe I am just that stupid. Maybe I should have seen this coming. God, I am so dumb. What an idiot! I hate him!"

I let her rage, knowing that she had a right to be upset and to express herself. She continued on, and it was like watching a self-esteem train wreck in slow motion.

"I mean, I am the idiot. What an idiot I am, like he could ever really love me. Why would I even believe that for a second? I am never able to make my relationships work. I am so stupid. Oh, God, what am I gonna do? I should call him. After I eat this ice cream. I am going to get really fat and not care about dating ever again. Yeah, I'm gonna eat and eat until there is no more ice cream left in the world. Oh, my God, I can't do that, I will never find a date. I am chunky as it is, can you imagine if I got fatter? Oh, my God, I would kill myself. That is it, I am not going to do this, and I am going to finally get in shape. Where is that coupon for the gym membership? I put it somewhere. . . ."

"Stop!" I yelled. I had reached my saturation point in

watching her spiral so deeply into the Language of Fat. I continued, "Enough! You are going in a million directions now, wanting to make the pain go away. Wanting to make excuses for his behavior. But you can't fix it right now. You just have to feel it. You can cry and scream and even call him names. But you can't speak the Language of Fat about yourself."

My screaming seemed to remind her that I wouldn't let her continue to berate herself.

After a few long moments of grieving, she picked her head up high and said, "I'm hungry. Let's go out to dinner." I was hungry too and happy that she had heard me.

We didn't always speak like this. For a while we were diet buddies and always connected by our shared obsessive thoughts. That night I felt like we had beaten the Language of Fat at its own game.

We were making our way toward the door when my friend remembered she had left her cell phone on the dresser. As she passed her hall mirror, I watched her take a look at her body. She grabbed the phone, and as she made her way back, she passed the hall mirror again. This time she stopped for one second more to look at her body. And one second was all she needed.

"Are you sure this doesn't make my butt look big?" she asked.

She wasn't teasing. I wish she had been. I didn't know what to say. Instead, I just stood there watching her scrutinize and focus on her body. I was fully in awe at just how intoxicating this language can be.

In the one second she stood before that mirror, time spiraled backward a dozen years to the time when we would have been studying our butts in the mirror, pulling apart and examining every inch of our appearance. In spite of all the hard emotional truths we shared that night and all the progress we had made, the Language of Fat still reared its ugly head.

> *Life is not what it's supposed to be.*
> *It's what it is. The way you cope with*
> *it is what makes the difference.*
> —Virginia Satir

Progress, Not Perfection

Rebuilding self-esteem doesn't come with a set of instructions. While you begin decoding the Language of Fat in your life, you will continue to hear people speak it all around you. Perhaps more so now than ever before, because now you have a heightened sensitivity to it. However, every single second of the day you get a chance to decide whether or not to engage in that language. And it is in those individual moments that you can take action to not be a conscious carrier of this destructive dialogue.

What happens once you've done all this work and are trying to engage in a new language, but the people you care most about are still on a totally different wavelength? How do you help a friend who is still speaking the Language of Fat? How do you even try to preserve an ounce of self-love in a world hell-bent on telling you that you are worthless if you aren't skinny, pretty, and slim?

Dear Jess,

Don't you ever just look in the mirror and think to yourself, "My butt is so huge!" or ever catch yourself saying, "I feel fat!" Don't you still get plagued by self-doubt and negative thoughts even after a long time of recovery? If not, what is your secret?

—Angelina

If you can remember that recovery is a process, not a product, then you can look at your own recovery from speaking the Language of Fat in small and meaningful ways.

- Do you spend more days without speaking the Language of Fat than you did previously in your life? **Victory!**
- Do you speak up when you have someone dear to you try to speak the Language of Fat? **Victory!**
- Do you recognize the messages in the media around you? **Victory!**
- Do you spend more time writing down your thoughts and feelings, and expanding your vocabulary to include words of emotion and feeling? **Victory!**
- Do you choose to treat yourself more kindly than you did before? **Victory!**

Rejecting negative thoughts in favor of more powerful ones is a victory. By amassing new coping tools, you will arm yourself to react differently, feel differently, think differently, speak differently, and act differently.

Let me be the first to paint you the most realistic picture of recovery that I can muster. It is not perfect. And neither are you. Just because you have adapted new coping skills doesn't mean you are exempt from all the same triggers, frustrations, failures, and challenges as everyone else.

> *And the day came when the risk to remain tight in a bud was more painful than the risk it took to blossom.* —Anaïs Nin

Dear Jess,

I have been trying really hard to not speak the Language of Fat around my girlfriends. Instead of talking about weight, I will ask them to share what they are feeling. But there are some days where that is just so hard to do. It seems they are bonding more over speaking about it together, and I'm feeling left out. I feel like I am the only one thinking about this language, and now that has become my identity in our group. For instance, when we are hanging out and someone says, "God, I need to lose weight!" or "Look how flabby my stomach has gotten," I feel like everyone turns their heads to me to see how I will respond. I just don't know if I have the energy to always walk my talk.

—Gail

Sometimes it can seem to be easier to forget everything you have learned about the Language of Fat and go back to bonding over mutual disdain for your bodies. After all, you may have upset a pattern of bonding within your tribe by choosing to be conscious of the language or taking action. Are your girlfriends friends for a lifetime—or friends for a moment in time? Are they women who have the potential to grow with you? Can you sit down with them and clear the air?

Just because you choose to eschew the Language of Fat in your life doesn't mean you are doomed to live life as a social pariah. Instead, it can mean:

- That your relationships can be more multifaceted and genuine.
- That you can grow into a richer relationship with yourself and feel invigorated by knowing your emotions, dreams, and desires.
- That you are willing to be part of the change and solution.
- That you are willing to take sincere and meaningful steps to evaluate your body image and examine where it rules, sidetracks, or interferes with areas of your life.

Truth be told, your skills may get rusty. You may need to gather more tools for your toolbox, but you are not in danger of losing the clarity and lessons you have experienced and earned thus far. You can't lose the progress you have achieved.

Dear Jess,

What can a woman do to preserve her self-love in such an insane world?

If I walk down the street, I am bombarded with magazine covers of overly airbrushed prepubescent girls, most of them with boob jobs or nose jobs, and if I walk into a store, I am bombarded with clothing cut to fit a small child, not a grown woman. Then, when I go to a club or restaurant with my friends, I inevitably will be bombarded with conversation about how much people weigh, and then when I come home to the respite of my house, I am bombarded with TV show after TV show shouting at me to be smaller, thinner, and prettier!

All of these makeover shows make me sick. All of these programs where women go on TV to find love make me even sicker. What is happening to us? Why are we never happy right where we are? And what are we supposed to do about this? There are those of us who are tired of hating ourselves and hating other women—we want this to end!

—An Actionist in Training

You need to get creative with ways to combat the Language of Fat and all the messaging that accompanies it.

Weapons for Fighting the Language of Fat

- Get your friends to put up signs on their bathroom mirrors that say NEGATIVE BODY TALK NOT ALLOWED!

- When you sit down with each other to eat or hang out, make a point to start off talking about the one thing that has gone *well* in your day, rather than sitting down and complaining.

- Try to make sure you all do at least one loving thing for yourselves each week, even if it is just writing in a gratitude journal for five minutes.

- Collect a dollar each time someone uses the Language of Fat. At the end of the month give the money to a charity.

- You can take large or small steps. You can create your own style of action. The most important thing is that you do *something*. And that you continue to do it until you feel or experience results. Once you have decoded the language, recognized where and when and how it is spoken in your life, and made the decision to do something about it, you are more than halfway there. The other half is living with the tools, acting with them as much as you can, and continuing to challenge the way you think, speak, and act.

When all is said and done, I can promise you this: You will no longer feel enslaved by a way of thinking and speaking that reduces you to a size, a weight, or a carbohydrate. You will no longer have to form relationships based on condemning conversation or humiliating gossip. You will no longer have to stay stuck in unhealthy patterns, and you will no longer have to sabotage your health, wealth, family, relationships, and career by speaking the Language of Fat.

> *We write our destiny; we become*
> *what we do.* —Madame Chiang Kai-shek

TAKE ACTION

1. You will still encounter the Language of Fat all around you. Don't be surprised and don't get discouraged.

2. Continue to decode this language and make small, sincere steps of progress in your everyday life. You have the choice moment to moment whether you will speak this language or not.

3. Remember that your recovery is progress, not a product. This is not a contest to see who can do it perfectly, this is your life. It will ebb and flow, and you will make mistakes. You will also have triumphs, so don't forget to celebrate, too!

4. Get creative in the ways you take action.

   a. Post notes on your mirrors barring any negative body talk.
   b. Collect money from your friends each time one of you begins to speak the Language of Fat, and then donate the money to a charity.
   c. Begin each gabfest with your friends by confessing something that has gone well in your day!

5. Above all else, do something. Take action and continue to do so until you see results.

Chapter Twelve

"Sorry, I Don't Speak That Language!"

Most commonly heard:
As a response to someone speaking the Language of Fat.

Translation(s):
Can mean any of the following, but is not limited to:

"I am not gonna go there with you and bond over whose butt is bigger or who ate more at lunch. I believe we deserve better than that!"

"I refuse to speak the Language of Fat. Instead, I want to engage in a more meaningful and authentic conversation."

"I am done talking diets and I am through believing my life begins five pounds from now. In order to speak with me, you'll have to address me in language that is clear and affirming. I don't play this game anymore."

Change *Will* Happen

It won't happen overnight. It may not even happen by next year. But change most certainly can happen. The Language of Fat is a cultural adaptation to societal messaging. And since you are all card-carrying members of society, you can choose to change this language. All it takes is the decision to become more aware of the language you speak, the thoughts you think, and the actions you take.

?? Where There's a Will . . . ???????????

- Are you willing to look deeper, dig deeper, and commit deeper?
- Are you willing to stretch out of your comfort zone and grow?
- Are you willing to let go and release the past?
- Are you willing to relinquish control over the future?
- Are you willing to embrace the life you have now, not five pounds from now?

Learning a New Language

After having spent time decoding the Language of Fat, I ran into a situation where it became obvious that I had to practice a new replacement language.

I was walking to my car after watching a night of amateur stand-up at a comedy club when I heard a voice yell to me from across the garage: "Jessica, wait up!" It was my new friend, Candice.

Candice was a performer and comedienne. She was incredibly funny and engaging, but her humor was based on self-deprecation. In her act she told a slew of fat jokes about herself. I could tell this had become her shtick, and I imagine it was because if she told the joke first and was laughing at herself, then no one could make fun of her.

She caught up to me and said, "I know we've been meaning to get together, and I wanted to invite you to a poker party I'm having next weekend."

"Awesome," I replied. "I've been learning how to play Texas Hold 'Em, and I'm ready to test my skills."

"Well, actually, the poker part is just a cover-up for what we really want to do—which is to get together and eat great food. I'm calling it a 'Big Girls' poker night, and I'd love for you to come!"

I thought I had misheard her.

"What kind of poker night did you say it was?"

"We're calling it a 'Big Girls' poker night. You know, a night where some big girls can come over and eat and drink what they'd like."

"Oh," I said, not quite sure how to process this information. "I usually do eat and drink what I like, whether I am playing poker or not. So I'm curious, why are you calling it a 'Big Girls' poker night?"

"I just thought it would be fun for all us big girls to get together and snack on whatever we'd like without worrying about it, since usually most of us are on diets during the week. Well, I am, anyway. And I have a great group of big ol' girl-friends who all love to hang out together and talk about . . . you know . . . girl stuff and . . . eat."

Okay, I said to myself.

1. Did she just call me a "big girl"?
2. Did she just invite me to a group binge disguised as a poker party?
3. Did she just call me a "big girl"?

The way I saw it, I had a few options:

A. I could just say thank you, tell her I would stop by, get in my car, and drive home, then never show up at her party and avoid her at all future social engagements.
B. I could just smile politely, chalk it up to an extremely awkward social faux pas, and tell no one that I was invited to a gorgefest at Candice's house.
C. I could begin blaming my body and allow Candice's invitation to a "Big Girls" poker night swim in my head all night (and probably the next day) with the word "big" especially playing on repeat, and subsequently summoning all the leftover body-loathing in my system.
D. I could get angry that someone felt they had the license to make a statement and judgment about me by the way they thought I looked.

I repeated my choices over and over again in my head. Ignore it, self-loathe about it, feel embarrassed, feel disappointed, or feel angry. Hmmm . . . none of them seemed like the choice I wanted to make.

Instead, something inside me said, *"Speak up, say something,"* not in a demeaning way but in defense of who I am and *my right to get through one day without having to hear another woman speak the Language of Fat.*

Tonight, silence would equal consent. And tonight, I refused to stay silent.

"So what do you think?" she said to me, completely unaware of my intense inner dialogue. "Do you think you're up for it next weekend?"

"No," I said.

"No?" she repeated, kind of shocked.

"No, Candice, I'm sorry but I am not interested, and I'll tell you why. With all due respect, I am not interested in going to a party where you would assign anyone the label of being a 'big girl.' I don't speak that language."

And that was it. My inner dialogue had become an outer dialogue.

"I don't speak the Language of Fat, and I don't choose to label anyone, especially myself, by their body shape or size. I appreciate your thinking of me. If you were inviting me to hang out and play poker with a group of diverse and lovely women, that would be appealing. But the fact that this night would give some women the excuse to eat 'forbidden' foods sounds unhealthy to me. I no longer bond with women over the size of our bodies. And speaking of bodies: Mine is none of your business. So next time don't assume that I would be okay with that label."

The words flew off my tongue with the eloquence that usually accompanies those daydreams where you get to say everything you want in your perfect fantasy confrontation. I didn't raise my voice. I stated the facts as they were—I no longer spoke the Language of Fat, and I wasn't going to pretend that I did.

Candice apologized profusely. She was embarrassed, and I could tell that I ran the risk of never connecting with her again. That was a risk I was willing to take. Yes, my ego was bruised by her offer to include me in her weekend bingefest. I wasn't sure why, and quite frankly I didn't need to figure that out. I didn't need to justify or qualify any of her intentions. All that I was responsible for was my response. I found it liberating to say what I felt and not allow another interaction to be poisoned by an assumption about my relationship to my body. I'm sure she thought she was being kind by inviting me, but I had spent years betraying my body's confidence and not defending its honor. That night everything changed. I chose to take action. I found my strength in these six words: "Sorry, I don't speak that language."

It was something I neither planned nor spent a lot of time practicing. But when I said those words, they opened up a world of possibility for me. They allowed me to access the truth and speak it.

More than anything, I realized that those six words could replace another six words that I had used often in the past: "Do I look fat in this?"

We could call it an even exchange, but it wouldn't be true. I was giving up six damaging words belonging to the Language of Fat and putting in their place six clarifying and empowering words belonging to my new language, the Language of Self-Love.

Life itself is the proper binge. —Julia Child

The Language of Self-Love

There are many ways to begin changing the Language of Fat into a Language of Self-Love, and not all of them require awkward confrontations in parking garages. You can take small steps toward annihilating this belief system in your life. When you think and speak differently, you will naturally act differently. Perhaps you will discover that an abundant amount of time has opened up in your life for you to connect with your family and friends. Perhaps you will find that your general outlook on life feels lighter because you are spending less time with condemning thoughts swirling in your head. Perhaps you will actually learn to love the body you were born with and spend more time using it to be active and alive in the world versus shut off and hid away. And perhaps you can greatly impact those around you by just being you, and by walking your talk. Wouldn't that be a gift?

Disappointing another to be true to yourself. Can you do it? It goes against our entire good-girl socializing and challenges us to really stick up for ourselves, often the last person we would ever defend. But if we don't do it, who will?

Replacing the Language of Fat with the Language of Self-Love means that you are willing to do what it takes to no longer demean, debase, and distract yourself with punishing thoughts and actions. It is recognition of a life worth living . . . as is. And when you take these slow and steady steps toward change, your whole world can and will open up.

Speaking the Language of Self-Love doesn't mean that your life has to become one psychobabble moment after the other. Instead, it can merely mean that you are waking up, becoming aware, and taking action on your own behalf. It means that you are creating a world where women don't have to be cruel to their bodies just because it fulfills a pattern of the past.

Take Action: Small Steps

1. Become aware that there is a Language of Fat and learn how to decode it.
2. Choose to not buy a magazine or watch a TV show because of the kinds of images and messaging it promotes.
3. Buy a magazine or watch a TV show to demonstrate support of the kinds of images and messages it promotes.
4. Stop laughing at fat jokes.
5. Write a letter to a studio, network, or company that is creating a product that is degrading to women.
6. Write a letter to your political leaders asking them to make health care for serious mental health issues like eating disorders more affordable and accessible.
7. Refuse to believe that your self-worth lies in the size of your jeans.
8. Do not nod in agreement or smile politely when someone is demeaning themselves about their weight.
9. Throw out the scale, diet books, and anything else that reminds you of restriction, shame, blame, and guilt
10. Read things, buy things, look at things that make you feel good about yourself.

Take Action: Big Steps

1. Choose to no longer stay silent when you witness someone speaking the Language of Fat.
2. No longer talk to your friends about dieting, weight loss, or how fat they are.
3. Watch the way you talk about your own body in front of children.

4. Stop describing people by what they look like.

5. Speak in clear, affirming language that says what you really mean.

6. Don't be afraid to say what you really mean!

7. Let your friends and family know that you have declared your house or apartment a "no body talk" zone.

8. Keep a journal or notebook and take inventory of your thoughts, feelings, and actions. Make a list and decide what small steps you can take every day to move you toward a life of living now, not five pounds from now.

9. Be willing to disappoint another to be true to yourself.

10. Continually take small steps of action whenever you can, where you can.

The man who removes a mountain begins by carrying away small stones.
—William Faulkner

Final Thoughts

- Are you content being a slave to your scale and the restrictive thoughts you have about your body?
- Are you content being distracted by all of the things you must consume and own in order to be worthy?
- Are you content spending hours, days, weeks, and even years of your life in shallow conversations about fat grams and diet pills?

What Does It Mean?

Q. Does speaking the Language of Self-Love mean you can never aim to lose weight again?

A. No. Your body is none of my business. Whether you choose to shift your physical form through increased activity and more loving eating habits is completely up to you. Just be clear that you aren't putting off living today for a number on the scale tomorrow. I'd love to know less about people's diets and more about their hearts.

Q. Does speaking the Language of Self-Love mean you won't be able to bond with your girlfriends?

A. I hope not! You can create friendships that are long lasting and have nothing to do with body size.

I am still learning. —Michelangelo

It's Who You Love and How You Love That Matters

Sometimes a major life lesson comes careening at you when you least expect it. It has the power and capacity to lift your focus from the daily details to the bigger picture. It has the force to eradicate all of your surface complaining and drag you deep beneath the surface to clarity and truth. This is what happened when I said good-bye to my grandma Mollie. After ninety-one years of loving laughter and heartfelt generosity on this planet, her time was drawing to a close. As we stood around my grandma's bed holding her hand and saying our good-byes, I noticed something that rocked my world. I was staring face-to-face at the final moments of someone's life.

And the focus wasn't on what she weighed or what she ate or how much money she had in the bank. It wasn't on what size pants she wore, or how many trophies she had earned. No, the focus wasn't on her looks, her possessions, or even her career.

The focus was on who she loved and how she loved.

All that mattered was love. The love we felt for her as her family. The love she gave to us as a mother, wife, sister, friend, and grandmother. It was about how big she loved and how boldly she loved. It was about how many people she touched with her love and about carrying on the legacy of love in our own lives.

All the other trappings disappeared. She was showing me even in the passing on of her life that nothing is more important than who you love and how you love.

And in that moment I promised to apply this lesson, and love myself first.

If I wasn't treating myself with love, where did I think it was going to come from? The thoughts of it magically appearing when I shrank my body or attained whatever status I was seeking were all illusory. I realized that I had to do the work. The hard, emotional, sometimes unpopular work of changing my thoughts, my language, and my actions.

You can decode the Language of Fat and replace it with a Language of Self-Love.

You can choose to be the very best woman you can be in your everyday life. And you can make a commitment to understand that this is a process, a well-earned and often-times long process.

If I truly did have superhero powers, I would focus them on creating a society where women don't bond over the Language of Fat. Where girls don't fear growing into women's bodies. And where women and men can communicate their feelings, thoughts, and emotions with ease.

So, until those powers (and the really cute superhero outfit that comes with it) are passed on to me, I guess I will just continue to live the very best life I can. Choosing to live it now, not five pounds from now.

Won't you join me?

Action may not always bring happiness, but there is no happiness without action.
—Benjamin Disraeli

TAKE ACTION

1. There are many ways to take action toward abstaining from the Language of Fat. Refer to the "Take Action" lists (see pages 196–197) and add some more of your own.

2. Remember that small steps of action can lead to big change.

3. Try replacing the Language of Fat with the Language of Self-Love.

4. Speak up! And be willing to disappoint another to be true to yourself.

5. Focus on *who* you love and *how* you love.

6. Start by loving you!

AFTERWORD

There were so many great stories and e-mails that didn't make it into this book but are captured in my heart forever. I want to hear from you, so please, continue to send me your thoughts and experiences and know that we are all taking small steps of action together to make great change in the world. If something in this book has stirred you and you feel you may need additional professional help, please contact the Eating Disorders Association, www.edauk.com, or call the helpline on 0845 634 1414 in the UK for a referral in your area. For additional resources and information, visit my Web site at www.jessicaweiner.com.

ACKNOWLEDGMENTS

It takes a village to raise a writer.

And a really special village to raise a healthy, empowered woman.

My love and gratitude go out to:

My parents: "Darcy" and "Roy," I couldn't love you more if I tried. It is because of you that I am able to stand tall and proud, and it is literally because of you that I could write this book. Thanks for lending me the upstairs space and for the love of my cute "Moolie Dog." We make a great team!

My amazing sister: Sherman, I am so blessed to be your best friend and "little" sister. You are a bright light in my life. I love you.

My right and left hands: Sharon Newport, your friendship and dedication are such gifts! Thanks for holding down the fort, "Parallax West Coast."

My No. 11 partner: Jillian Fleer, you have taught me the meaning of heart, hope, partnership, and patience! Thank you for seeing me and believing in me. And thank you to Sid and Daria for being such beautiful souls in the world.

The best group of friends a girl could have: "Kenny Joe from Kokomo," my "Sweet Angel" Jenny Ward, and "Boo" Richardson, thank you for allowing me to be truly who I am and loving me for it.

My N.Y. wife: Jennifer Bergstrom, thank you for supporting this voice and vision, and sharing with me your sweetness and brilliance.

My editor, pep talker, and all-around word whiz: Elizabeth Bracken, thank you for helping me give birth! Your kindness, friendship, and insight were essential.

My Simon Spotlight Entertainment superstars: Jennifer Robinson, Jennifer Slattery, Tricia Boczkowski, Julie Amitie, Patrick Price, Katherine Devendorf, Lauren Forte, Steve Kennedy, and Cara Bedick, thank you for letting the world know about this book. And thank you to Greg Stadnyk and Russell Gordon for the kick-ass cover!

My protector: Keith Fleer, thank you for your immense fairness, persistence, love, and support!

My dynamic duo: Julie Kane-Ritsch and Ellen Goldsmith-Vein, thanks for the support and the hookup!

My power players at WMA: Thank you to Evan Warner, Scott Agostoni, John Ferriter, Jonathan Pecarsky, and Cameron Kadison.

My intern extraordinaire: Sally Cohen-Cutler, thank you for your insane work ethic, energy, and enthusiasm. Can I clone you?

My support team: Steve and Roseanne Nenninger, thank you for always having my back. Derek Simms, thank you for making me cyber-ready. My Grandpa Phil for supporting me from afar. And Kathleen DiPerna, for the marathon artichoke sessions of truth!

My inspirations: To my little cousins, and powerful women in their own right—Anna, Jenna, Haley, and Molly, may you never speak the Language of Fat!

My mentors and wise women: The delicious Emme and Leeza Gibbons, thank you for walking your talk and showing me the way.

My extremely amazing audience: Thank you so much for writing in, opening up, and sharing your stories. Each e-mail you send and phone call I receive fills me up in immeasurable ways. I am doing this for you, and I thank you for your support!

And finally, a special heavenly shout out to my writing angels, Grandma Mollie, Grandma Leona, and Grandpa Michael—look, I wrote it down . . . again!